The Risk of School Rampage

Other Palgrave Pivot titles

Kevin Jefferys: The British Olympic Association: A History

James E. Will: A Contemporary Theology for Ecumenical Peace

Carrie Dunn: Female Football Fans: Community, Identity and Sexism

G. Douglas Atkins: T.S. Eliot: The Poet as Christian

Raphael Sassower: The Price of Public Intellectuals

Joanne Westwood, Cath Larkins, Dan Moxon, Yasmin Perry and Nigel Thomas: Participation, Citizenship and Intergenerational Relations in Children and Young People's Lives: Children and Adults in Conversation

Jonathan Grix: Leveraging Legacies from Sports Mega-Events: Concepts and Cases

Edward Webb: Media in Egypt and Tunisia: From Control to Transition?

Dayan Jayatilleka: The Fall of Global Socialism: A Counter-Narrative from the South

Linda Lawrence-Wilkes and Lyn Ashmore: The Reflective Practitioner in Professional Education

Anna-Brita Stenström: Teenage Talk: From General Characteristics to the Use of Pragmatic Markers in a Contrastive Perspective

Divya Wodon, Naina Wodon, and Quentin Wodon: Membership in Service Clubs: Rotary's Experience

Robert C. Robinson: Justice and Responsibility—Sensitive Egalitarianism

Alison Heron-Hruby and Melanie Landon-Hays (editors): Digital Networking for School Reform: The Online Grassroots Efforts of Parent and Teacher Activists

R. A. Houston: The Coroners of Northern Britain c. 1300–1700

Christina Slade: Watching Arabic Television in Europe: From Diaspora to Hybrid Citizens

F. E. Knowles, Jr.: The Indian Law Legacy of Thurgood Marshall

Louisa Hadley: Responding to Margaret Thatcher's Death

Kylie Mirmohamadi: The Digital Afterlives of Jane Austen: Janeites at the Keyboard

Rebeka L. Maples: The Legacy of Desegregation: The Struggle for Equality in Higher Education

Stijn Vanheule: Diagnosis and the DSM: A Critical Review

James DeShaw Rae: Analyzing the Drone Debates: Targeted Killing, Remote Warfare, and Military Technology

Torben Bech Dyrberg: Foucault on the Politics of *Parrhesia*

Bernice M. Murphy: The Highway Horror Film

Jolene M. Sanders: Women in Narcotics Anonymous: Overcoming Stigma and Shame

The Risk of School Rampage: Assessing and Preventing Threats of School Violence

Eric Madfis
Assistant Professor, University of Washington, Tacoma, USA

palgrave macmillan

THE RISK OF SCHOOL RAMPAGE
Copyright © Eric Madfis, 2014.
Softcover reprint of the hardcover 1st edition 2014 978-1-137-40165-6

All rights reserved.

First published in 2014 by
PALGRAVE MACMILLAN®
in the United States—a division of St. Martin's Press LLC,
175 Fifth Avenue, New York, NY 10010.

Where this book is distributed in the UK, Europe and the rest of the world, this is by Palgrave Macmillan, a division of Macmillan Publishers Limited, registered in England, company number 785998, of Houndmills, Basingstoke, Hampshire RG21 6XS.

Palgrave Macmillan is the global academic imprint of the above companies and has companies and representatives throughout the world.

Palgrave® and Macmillan® are registered trademarks in the United States, the United Kingdom, Europe and other countries.

ISBN 978-1-349-48646-5   ISBN 978-1-137-39928-1 (eBook)
DOI 10.1057/9781137399281

Library of Congress Cataloging-in-Publication Data is available from the Library of Congress.

A catalogue record of the book is available from the British Library.

First edition: 2014

www.palgrave.com/pivot

Contents

Preface	viii
1 Introduction	**1**
Research questions and background information on averted school rampage incidents	2
Explaining and reacting to school rampage	6
School rampage as a social problem	6
The causes of school rampage	7
Averted school rampage	8
Responding to rampage—current school disciplinary and security practices	11
Responding to rampage—violence risk assessment	13
Understanding school criminalization and risk assessment as actuarial justice	18
2 Assessing the Substance and Risk of Student Rampage Threats	**23**
Distinguishing threats, risks, plots, and genuine aversion	26
Examining the form and content of threats in averted rampage violence	27
Examining the levels of risk in averted rampage violence	29
Examining plots and planning in averted rampage violence	31

	Examining the notion of aversion in rampage violence	31
	The assessment of evidence in averted rampage violence	31
	Assessing the plot's detail	32
	Appraising the role of weaponry	38
	Assessing the role of personal and group characteristics	43
	Conclusion	54
3	**Confidence and Doubts about Assessing Averted Rampage Violence**	**56**
	Variations in confidence and doubt by risk assessment type	57
	Certainty based on a convergence of risk assessment criteria	58
	Certainty based on lack of threat assessment criteria	59
	Certainty based on threat assessment criteria in spite of deviation from profiles	62
	Remaining uncertainty despite risk assessment	63
	Conclusion	65
4	**Preventing School Rampage Violence through Student Bystander Intervention and Positive School Environments**	**69**
	School rampage violence prevention and the student code of silence	70
	Perceiving a diminished student code of silence since Columbine	74
	Weakening the code of silence through positive school climate	75
	Breaking the code of silence—interventions through leakage	78
	Indirectly informed bystanders	78
	Directly informed confidants	79
	Threatened targets	80
	Involved co-conspirators	80
	How interventions occurred and who was trusted	83

	Following the code of silence—the persistence of bystander inaction	84
	Implications of findings	87
	Conclusion	90
5	Summary of Findings, Policy Implications, and Future Research	95
	Summary and implications of findings	96
	Suggested areas for future research	100
6	Methodological Appendix	104
	Operationalizing school rampage and averted threat	105
	Research design and sample	108
	Complications of relying on the news media to build a sampling frame	113
	On qualitative methodology	114
	Generalizability in qualitative research	115

References 117

Index 140

Preface

Over the last few decades, school rampage shootings have taken multiple lives and caused widespread fear throughout the United States. During this same period, however, dozens of potential incidents have also been averted wherein student plots to kill multiple peers and faculty members came to the attention of authorities and thus were thwarted. This book investigates how such successes occurred, utilizing data gleaned from in-depth interviews conducted with 32 school and police officials (administrators, counselors, security and police officers, and teachers) who were directly involved in assessing and preventing what many perceived to be potential rampages at 11 public middle and high schools across the Northeastern United States. A multi-tiered method was employed to examine the process by which threats of rampage violence are assessed by school and police officials as well as how previous school rampage plots have been averted. Interview data about the 11 averted incidents were triangulated via news media reporting and legal documentation (such as court transcripts, arrest reports, and legal briefs) in order to verify concordance with and inconsistencies among the interviewees' accounts of their threat assessments and crime prevention practices.

The resultant data provide insight into the institutional cultures and practices that were involved in determining the magnitude of school rampage risks and ultimately enabling various potential attacks to be foiled. In addition, the findings also serve as a means through which to better understand contemporary perspectives on the fear, risk assessment, and criminalization of American youth. The way in which school authorities have reacted to the school rampage phenomenon reveals a great deal about our current justice mindset, which often views the identification, surveillance, and management of potentially dangerous individuals as the best approach to what is understood as the inevitability of crime. Subsequently, this research reveals the significant shortcomings and sometimes harmful consequences of contemporary risk assessment, violence prevention, and punishment practices prominent in American schools.

By examining averted incidents, this work addresses problematic gaps in school violence scholarship and reveals both practical implications for the assessment and prevention of school violence and significant theoretical insight regarding the causes and consequences of enhanced school discipline and security.

Broadly, this book explores perceptions of and reactions to threats of rampage school violence. In Chapter 1, readers will be introduced to the phenomenon of school rampage, the literature on the causes and reactions to prior incidents of school violence, and the field of violence risk assessment. This chapter will also situate the American reaction to school rampage in the broader social context of contemporary school disciplinary and security practices and will provide theoretical background for explaining recent developments though insights from the sociology of risk, actuarial justice, and neoliberal penality. The second chapter illustrates how school and police officials engage in violence risk assessment by examining the forms of evidence present when claims are made that a school rampage threat has been averted. After categorizing the forms of risk assessment that have been utilized, Chapter 3 addresses the extent to which and under what circumstances officials express confidence in their use of risk assessment. The fourth chapter covers the manner in which student threats of rampage violence have come to the attention of parents, police, and school authorities in order to be averted and considers the extent to which students have actually broken through a code of silence which discourages them from informing on their peers. In addition, as many contemporary school violence prevention practices (such as enhanced discipline and increased surveillance) were not found to play a decisive role in preventing these incidents, alternative approaches from restorative justice are suggested to improve school climates, and accordingly, to increase positive bystander behavior on the part of students. Chapter 5 presents a discussion of the findings as a whole along with the policy and theoretical implications that may be drawn from them and suggests areas for future research. Finally, Chapter 6 serves as a methodological appendix and addresses the research design of the project as well as the benefits and potential limitations of the study's methods.

1
Introduction

Madfis, Eric. *The Risk of School Rampage:
Assessing and Preventing Threats of School Violence.*
New York: Palgrave Macmillan, 2014.
DOI: 10.1057/9781137399281.0003.

Over the last ten years in the United States, there have been hundreds of school rampage plots that have successfully been averted (Daniels et al. 2007; O'Toole 2000; Trump n.d.). During this same period, however, American schools have prioritized discipline and security in a manner which has exaggerated the extent of school violence as a social problem and dramatically transformed public education as a social institution. In the wake of numerous highly publicized multiple-victim school homicides that occurred during the 1990s, American schools responded with massive changes to their disciplinary policies and security apparatuses. With the intention of preventing future rampage shootings, schools implemented increased security through school resource officers (hereafter, SROs), cameras, locked doors, and lockdown procedures, and expanded discipline via zero tolerance policies with mandatory arrests and school exclusions. This cluster of practices, which Hirshfield and Celinska (2011) have collectively referred to as "school criminalization," represent the fairly recent but pervasive incursion of law enforcement personnel, ideology, and technology into the school setting. In addition, many school officials and academics responded with a risk assessment approach by focusing upon the identification of potential school shooters through warning sign check lists, behavioral profiles, and threat assessments.

Whatever failures or successes these varied approaches have had with regard to fighting school crime or violence more generally, no prior scholarship has looked at the numerous cases of rampage plots which have actually been averted in order to discern if and when any of these developments have actually played a preventative role. In fact, with the exception of a few recent studies (Daniels et al. 2007; 2010; Larkin 2009; Pollack et al. 2008), social scientists possess almost no information on the rampage attacks which have been plotted and planned, but never came to fruition. Through their exploration, this study endeavors to understand not only how schools assess violent threats and construct risk generally and at times problematically, but also what social and individual forces have been at work to prevent instances of rampage violence from taking place.

Research questions and background information on averted school rampage incidents

Averted incidents of school rampage offer a unique opportunity for social scientific investigation. As there has been little empirical research on how previous rampage plots have been thwarted, most of the rhetorical arguments regarding how future attacks are to be prevented amount to mere speculation and rely on many problematic assumptions about the unlimited benefits and minimal consequences of enhanced school criminalization and risk assessment.

First, this book will explore the process by which schools engage in the risk assessment of their students. To what extent are school officials aware of various forms of violence risk assessment and what are their perspectives regarding the utility of these techniques? Which approaches are utilized for what purposes? What criteria do police and school officials deem most important in the assessment of student threat? How do school officials manage student threats and maintain a sense of safety in the school community? A second goal of this research was to ascertain how student threats of rampage violence have been successfully averted. In particular, how have these threats come to the attention of authorities? What role did risk assessment and the expansion of punitive discipline and enhanced security in schools play in the prevention of the rampage plots? What additional factors, policies, or procedures permitted the rampage to be averted?

My data reveal that, between the years 2000–2009, there were at least 195 averted incidents where student plots to kill multiple peers and faculty members came to the attention of authorities and thus were thwarted. I conducted in-depth interviews with 32 school and police officials (administrators, counselors, security and police officers, and teachers) directly involved in assessing and preventing potential rampages at 11 middle and high schools located across the Northeastern United States.

All of the 11 schools that granted me permission for interviews were public institutions. Nine were high schools, one was a middle school, and one was a junior/senior high school. Two were located in Pennsylvania, one was in New York, two were in New Jersey, three were in Massachusetts, and three were in Connecticut. All 11 schools were located in communities where the vast majority of residents were white. Six of these schools were located in suburban predominantly middle class communities, four of them were located in affluent suburban areas, and one school was in a lower middle class rural community (please consult Chapter 6 for additional demographic information about schools and their communities). In order to preserve the anonymity of participants, pseudonyms have been used for all individuals and schools, and no sources (whether news media reporting or legal documentation on specific cases) can be explicitly referenced or cited. This is consistent with how Daniels and his colleagues (2007; 2010; 2011) presented their findings on incidents of averted school rampage.

In the first case at Adams High School, a 16-year-old male student, who later admitted to making and exploding more than 40 bombs in the woods near his suburban home, sent videos of himself firing his father's guns and using the homemade explosives to a friend. The friend's mother notified the police, and numerous weapons, including two assault rifles, and detailed plans to commit a rampage attack at his school were seized from the teenager's bedroom.

The second case occurred at the affluent Blane High School, where several students came forward to inform administrators that one of their peers had brought explosives to school with him. When school officials searched this student's backpack, they discovered tennis balls filled with explosives. Later, police found four additional explosive devices at the student's home.

In the third incident, a 15-year-old student at Courtside High School stole three handguns and hundreds of rounds of ammunition from his father's safe. According to the best friend he entrusted to hold onto these weapons for him, he intended to use them in his plan to attack the school.

A fourth incident ended when three teenagers were arrested while walking down a street carrying an arsenal of weapons and thousands of rounds of ammunition, after failing in their attempt to steal a car. They intended to use the vehicle to embark on a killing spree throughout their town, including a massacre of students at Donovan High School who had teased them.

The fifth case involved three teenage students at Everton High School creating very detailed and threatening profiles on a social networking website. These profiles featured, among many other disturbing images and words, a digital countdown clock ticking down to the anniversary of the Columbine massacre and several communications and videos expressing the desire to kill lots of people.

Four students at Finley High School, in the sixth incident, were involved in elaborate planning and extensive training to commit a rampage attack at their school. Despite many attempts, these students were never able to attain their own firearms, but they did acquire BB guns, knives, axes, gunpowder, and several homemade explosives. When one of the conspirator's dedication to carrying out their deadly plans became in question, the other three plotters went to school authorities and blamed everything on their reluctant friend, though the complicity of the whole group was eventually revealed to the police.

In the seventh case, several students at the affluent Greenvale High School expressed serious concern to school administrators about one of their peers having what they perceived to be a hit list of the names of his current and former teachers written in his notebook. The student ultimately left the school voluntarily rather than facing expulsion.

The eighth incident entailed five students at a rural combined middle and high school, Hastings Jr/Sr High School, who made death threats against various members of the football team and other students on a social networking website. One of the threatened students informed his parents about the threats, and this parent, in turn, called the president of the school board to express concern. The school was shut down for the remainder of the week, and several students were suspended.

In case nine, a teacher and several students at affluent Iverson High School noticed threatening messages scribbled onto walls in a boys' bathroom stall and informed the school principal. An 18-year-old student was arrested and charged with threatening with a deadly device and disturbing a school assembly.

In the tenth case, a teacher at Jefferson Middle School saw one of her students, a 13-year-old girl, writing out a list of people she disliked on a piece of paper at the girl's desk and subsequently notified the school principal. As the paper was interpreted as a hit list, she was charged with making terrorist threats against her classmates, suspended indefinitely, and forced to undergo psychiatric evaluation.

In the final incident, the eleventh case, students at Kranston High School noticed a threatening message written on the wall in one of the boys' bathroom stalls. These students then informed teachers who in turn told the school principal and SRO about the written threat, but no one was ever found responsible.

Through the detailed investigation of these cases of averted rampage violence, my research explores how officials explain their concerns about violent threats, the process by which threats are assessed and notions of safety are maintained, and how previous school rampage plots have been averted. The resultant data provide insight into the school cultures, policies, and procedures that enabled rampage attacks to be foiled, but also are a means through which to better understand contemporary perspectives on the fear, risk assessment, and surveillance of American youth.

Therefore, the way in which school authorities have reacted to the school rampage phenomenon reveals a great deal about our contemporary justice mindset, which often views the identification, surveillance, and management of potentially dangerous individuals as the best approach to the inevitability of crime. As such, this research contains both practical implications for the assessment and prevention of school violence and significant theoretical insight regarding the causes and consequences of enhanced school discipline and security.

Explaining and reacting to school rampage

School rampage as a social problem

A dramatic series of mass killings took place in the late 1990s at several rural and suburban public middle and high schools across the United States. These events were highly publicized as they shocked the American public not only for their brutality, but because of the prior belief that such schools were "safe havens, free of the dangers of street crime" (Lawrence 2007: 147). That such violence could be perpetrated in middle and upper class school districts away from the plight of urban areas was seen as especially perplexing (Kimmel and Mahler 2003). Perhaps unsurprisingly, a great deal of empirical research has since been conducted on the phenomenon.

While the term school shooting has been defined and operationalized in almost countless ways by many different scholars, Newman et al. (2004: 50) can be credited with delineating the concept as "rampage school shootings" which "take place on a school-related public stage before an audience; involve multiple victims, some of whom are shot simply for their symbolic significance or at random; and involve one or more shooters who are students or former students of the school." While only a portion of school gun violence fit all of these criteria, many of the most publicized events during the last two decades conform to these specifics. In addition to the aforementioned rampage shootings, Muschert (2007: 62) has filled in this typological picture to form the accompanying school shooting categories of "mass murders" committed by older nonstudent perpetrators, "terrorist attacks" engaged in by individuals or groups to advance their political or ideological goals, "targeted shootings" that involve only specific preplanned victims, and the "government shootings" of student protesters.

Though the reaction to rampage school shootings may have constituted a moral panic in terms of the excesses in media coverage and the overzealous policy reforms that exaggerated their prevalence (Aitken 2001; Best 2002; Burns and Crawford 1999), these events did genuinely occur with greater frequency in middle and high schools in the late 1990s (Fox, Levin, and Quinet 2005) and then on college campuses in the late 2000s (Fox and Savage 2009), and dozens of plots to commit such heinous crimes continue to be revealed and preempted every year (Trump n.d.). Likewise, since the April 1999 Columbine massacre, school shooters in nations around the world have turned to this infamous American case for homicidal inspiration (Larkin, 2009; Madfis and Levin 2013). Rare as these events may be, such incidents warrant serious concern for, when they do occur, they not only cause multiple casualties but leave many survivors and bystanders with post-traumatic stress (James 2009: Schwarz and Kowalski 1991) and create extensive fear among the larger public (Altheide 2009; Burns and Crawford 1999; Harding et al. 2002). In the literature review to follow, the extant scholarship on completed and averted school rampages will be discussed, followed by a review of the current state of discipline, security, and surveillance that has become so widely pervasive in American public schools since the turn of the 21st century and which has resulted, at least in part, as a reaction to the problem of school rampage shootings.

The causes of school rampage

Due to the prolific fear and extensive publicity which school rampages received in the late 1990s, the bulk of social science research has focused on this particular form of school shooting (Muschert 2007). The etiology of school rampage shootings has been explored by a vast array of academics ranging from sociologists and criminologists to anthropologists, social workers, psychologists, and psychiatrists. Often, scholars have brought one particular causal factor to the fore, whether it is an individual deficiency, the school or community context, or the larger socio-cultural background.

At the individual-level, some have focused upon the depression, mental illness, and personality disorders of said killers (Langman 2009a; Langman 2009b; McGee and DeBernardo 1999). Others have stressed the role played by negative relationships with peers, such as victimization through bullying (Burgess et al. 2006; Kimmel and Mahler 2003;

Klein 2012; Larkin 2007; Leary et al. 2003; Levin and Madfis 2009; Meloy et al. 2001; Newman et al. 2004). Both the exclusionary nature of teenage cliques (Larkin 2007; Lickel et al. 2003) and the cohesion of intolerant homogeneous communities (Aronson 2004; Newman et al. 2004) have been implicated in previous rampage attacks. Finally, at the macro-sociological level, various researchers have clarified the role that masculinity (Kimmel and Mahler 2003; Mai and Alpert 2000) and the widespread accessibility and acceptance of gun culture (Glassner 2010; Haider-Markel and Joslyn 2001; Lawrence and Birkland 2004; Webber 2003) play in reinforcing and legitimizing violent solutions. Of late, scholars (such as Henry 2009; Hong et al. 2011; Levin and Madfis 2009; Muschert and Peguero 2010) have attempted to fuse these disparate etiological concerns to achieve a more multi-faceted, holistic, and cross-disciplinary understanding of the causes of school rampage across the micro, meso, and macro levels of analysis.

Averted school rampage

Despite the breadth of research and theorizing on school rampages, few studies have addressed attacks which have been planned yet have not come to fruition. Whereas incidents of school violence that have resulted in multiple fatalities and injuries are often extensively investigated by numerous parties in the government, the justice system, and the media, far less information exists about "near misses" (Verlinden et al. 2000: 28). Pollack et al. (2008: 9) pointed out that:

> few [schools] track threats made against other students or the school (especially if the event did not result in official law enforcement intervention). The result of this failure to collect and maintain records regarding threats is that very little is known about the extent or nature of the problem.

Some academics have tried to make up for the lack of a comprehensive database by gathering their own samples. O'Toole (2000) first noted the importance of studying averted school rampages, and several scholars (Larkin 2009; Newman et al. 2004) have since compiled incidents of averted rampages but only tangentially discussed them. Those interested in advancing the field of violence risk assessment (Borum et al. 2010; Cornell 2003; Cornell et al. 2004; Cornell and Sheras 2006; Fein et al. 2002; Jimerson et al. 2005; O'Toole 2000; Randazzo et al. 2006; Reddy et al. 2001; Pollack et al. 2008) have focused upon understanding averted school attacks as have Langman (2005) and Madfis (2014a), but the lion's share of scholarship on the topic to date has been conducted by Daniels and his colleagues (Daniels et al. 2007; 2010; Daniels and Bradley 2011).

Daniels and his colleagues (2007) first completed a content analysis of 30 school rampages which were thwarted in 21 states sometime between October 2001 and October 2004. From newspaper accounts, the authors reported data on the details of the plot, how the plot was discovered, what steps were taken by the school and law enforcement once the plot was revealed, and the legal outcomes of the incidents. They discovered that the majority of violent schemes had planned for the attack to occur in public high schools, though several targeted public elementary and middle schools and one was aimed at a private school. In half of the incidents, one student acting alone was implicated, while two to six students were accused in the other half. Guns were the most frequent intended weapon for plotters, though bombs, knives, and swords were mentioned in the reporting of other incidents. The majority of plotters, 65%, communicated their fatal plans to others, with 30% doing so via email or paper notes, 20% verbally informing others, and 15% admitting guilt when questioned by police. Rampage plots were uncovered in a variety of ways. The most common method was other students coming forward to inform school or police officials. This was often a result of plotters informing, and in some cases unsuccessfully recruiting, their peers, but students who had overheard rumors or themselves been personally threatened also came forward. Other plots were averted by alert school administrators whose suspicions were aroused by rumors or irregular student behavior, and in some cases, school staff overheard the conversations of plotters. Still others were prevented by police who were alerted to rumors or found notes or emails which revealed the threat. Two massacres were avoided when the plots were discovered as a result of the students being investigated for other crimes, and one well-developed plan was preempted only 30 minutes before it was to be carried out. Schools responded to discovered plots in numerous ways. Students involved in plots were usually suspended or expelled and also often arrested. Schools also responded by notifying parents and students, making counseling available, conducting internal investigations, calling the police, enhancing school security, and evacuating, searching, and/or closing down the school. Less common school responses were to consider banning trench coats and to avoid doing anything to change the school's normal routine.

In his next stage of scholarship on this topic, Daniels and his colleagues (2010) conducted interviews with school personnel at four American schools where shooting rampages were averted. The goal of this research was to better understand what roles school officials felt they played in preventing the rampage incidents, what reasons they attributed to the successful outcome, and what advice they would offer to other schools. The research design for this project was ostensibly qualitative and, while the authors categorized respondents' interview data into helpful domains and core ideas, they then quantified the prevalence of these themes in a manner which subsequently sacrificed what could have been a more in-depth understanding of these themes. The study revealed that the most dominant domains represented in interviews were descriptions of school conditions that focused on: (1) securing safety and optimizing learning, (2) intervention descriptions about how plots were discovered, (3) discussions about crisis planning and preparation, (4) conversations regarding interpersonal relationships between staff and students, (5) debates about the relative merits of violence prevention efforts, and (6) problematic issues at the school which made dealing with the crisis more difficult. In their analysis, Daniels and his colleagues (2010: 88) concluded that anti-bullying programs were perceived to be the "most salient" method of preventing future rampages. Many school officials also believed that supportive and strong relationships between school staff and students encourage people to come forward with knowledge about threats, and that formal crisis planning that dictates specific roles helps to both prevent and respond to such potentially dangerous incidents.

The scholarship of Daniels and his colleagues contributed significant original knowledge about foiled school rampages through content analyses and interviews with school personnel. Little research, in contrast, has been conducted by interviewing the failed perpetrators themselves. Such a deficit similarly exists in research on completed school rampage killers and on mass murderers more generally, those who have killed numerous people in a single episode at one or more closely related locations (Fox and Levin 2011). Very few researchers have attained multiple interviews with successful mass killers, as Mullen (2004) and Vossekuil et al. (2002) constitute the only examples. However, Langman (2005: 25) wrote about his experiences with "potential school shooters in a locked psychiatric hospital." In this brief article, Langman described the differences between deniers, admitters, and intenders of school shootings. Deniers refute that they ever intended to do harm to others and minimize or contest any evidence which suggests otherwise. Admitters acknowledge their violent thoughts and sometimes quite detailed plans, but state that they never had any intention to carry them through. Intenders admit that they desire to, or may be at risk for carrying out a homicidal episode, though they may lack any semblance of a plan. This preliminary typology speaks to both the difficulty in assessing seriousness and the complexity inherent in predicting what people, especially teenagers, may do in the future.

Responding to rampage—current school disciplinary and security practices

The current state of school discipline, security, and surveillance does not resemble the American public schools of even a few decades ago. A regime of tighter social control has manifested itself in schools across the country through punitive zero tolerance disciplinary policies, the proliferation of police officers and surveillance cameras, and various forms of school security designed to prevent crime through environmental design. As a result, students are increasingly exposed to prison-like regimes of control (Hirschfield 2008; Kupchik 2010; Monahan and Torres 2010).

Zero tolerance disciplinary policies

One of the most frequently cited reactions to the various school shooting massacres of the late 1990s was the implementation of various zero tolerance disciplinary policies, which mandate strict penalties for student misbehavior regardless of individual or situational circumstances. Though the original formulation took the form of the 1994 Gun Free Schools Act which required schools to expel, for a minimum of one year, any student caught carrying a firearm in school, various states and individual school districts broadened the scope to include zero tolerance policies for aggressive behavior, possession of other objects deemed as weapons, and various controlled substances (Ayers et al. 2001). As a result, schools have expelled, suspended, or sent to alternative schools large numbers of students for sharing over-the-counter medications with their peers, for bringing utensils and toy weapons to school, some made of paper or plastic, to school grounds, or for making relatively questionable gestures or comments which have been deemed violent or threatening.

Skiba and Peterson (1999) documented several of the more egregious examples that showcased the "dark side of zero tolerance" spawned by fear of Columbine and other similar shootings. One particularly egregious incident involved the suspension of an 8-year-old child for pointing a chicken finger at a teacher and saying "Pow, pow, pow" (Times Wire Reports 2001). Though zero tolerance policies have been widely condemned by various academics (Ayers et al. 2001; Casella 2003; Skiba 2000), the American Bar Association (2001), and the American Psychological Association (APA Zero Tolerance Task Force 2008), these punitive policies persist. In 2009, a 6-year-old boy from Newark, Delaware was suspended for bringing his Cub Scouts camping utensil to lunch (Urbina 2009), and, in 2010, a 13-year-old female honor roll student in Houston, Texas was expelled and labeled a "terrorist" by the school's principal for pointing a "finger gun" in the general direction of one of her teachers ("Student Suspended" 2010).

Surveillance through the proliferation of school resource officers and security cameras

The last few decades have seen a massive increase in the surveillance of school students, whether that means through additional SROs officially stationed as police liaisons or security cameras which record student movements through school hallways, entrances, and exits. Whereas there were less than 100 police officers in American public schools at the end of the 1970s (Brady et al. 2007), there are now approximately 17,000 SROs working in public schools nationwide (Thurau and Wald 2010). Thus, 60% of teachers in suburban middle and high schools (and 67% of teachers in majority-black or Hispanic schools) reported armed police officers working at their schools (Public Agenda 2004).

Not unlike police officers in schools, security cameras were a rare sight 30 years ago anywhere but in prisons and retail establishments. They did not arrive in schools until the 1990s and, while urban school districts were the first to implement cameras, today wealthy suburban schools are usually the proud owners of the most sophisticated and expensive surveillance technology (Casella 2006). During the 1999–2000 school year, only 19% of all public high schools used security cameras to monitor their students (Dinkes et al. 2009: vii). By the 2007–2008 school year, 55% of all public schools (and 76.6% of all public high schools) possessed security cameras (Ruddy et al. 2010). While cameras may have numerous security and monitoring benefits, as well as the potential for various invasions of personal privacy, the security industry markets technological surveillance as an inevitable "way of the future" (Casella 2003: 88).

School security designed to prevent crime through environmental design

Part of a larger field referred to as Crime Prevention through Environmental Design (CPTED) influenced by Routine-Activities Theory (Felson 1994), attaining school safety via the use of architectural designs—such as large windows, skylights, and straight hallways to increase visibility—has become extremely lucrative. The advent of gates, specialized door locks, and the limiting of entry and exit to one location during school hours have similarly been adopted to secure areas in numerous school buildings (Casella 2006). Typically affluent communities prefer these environmental designs (as well as surveillance through police and cameras) to the daily use of metal detectors and random weapon searches. These latter invasive security measures are more commonly found in urban schools with predominantly minority students (Hirschfield 2010).

Responding to rampage—violence risk assessment

According to scholars documenting its origins, the field of violence risk assessment has advanced from early empirical studies in the 1970s that attempted to predict violence to a more complex, multi-disciplinary research literature which deals not only with the estimation and assessment of future violence potential, but also how best to manage and intervene with high-violence risk individuals (Andrade 2009). Knowledge gleaned from this field is frequently used by numerous practitioners, from "adult and juvenile courts, parole and probation departments, and correctional facilities, as well as for child protective services agencies, school departments, community mental health centers, and more" (Andrade, O'Neill, and Diener 2009: 3). While all methods of risk assessment engage in the "scientific effort to identify ways to improve estimates of future violence," the approaches vary substantially (Grisso 2009: xvi). Reddy and colleagues (2001) codified and categorized these varied approaches as profiling, guided professional judgment, automated decision making, and threat assessment.

Profiling

Profiling, often qualified as criminal profiling (Douglas et al. 1986; Kocsis 2007; Turvey 2008), behavioral profiling (Petherick 2006), or offender profiling (Canter and Youngs 2009; Keppel 2006; Palermo and Kocsis 2005), is practiced in a number of diverse forms but broadly refers to investigative techniques or assessment strategies used to identify current and potential offenders. In its original form developed by the FBI's Behavioral Science Unit, hypotheses regarding offenders' behavioral, demographic, and personality characteristics were generated from data left at crime scenes (Douglas et al. 1986). The realm of profiling has expanded, however, to include the "prospective identification of would-be criminals" wherein "the typical perpetrator of a particular type of crime—such as serial murder or school shootings—is compiled from characteristics shared by known previous perpetrators" (Reddy 2001: 161). This prototypical profile is then used to both identify the types of individuals likely to become perpetrators and to assess an individual's likelihood of future offending. To this end, the FBI (Band and Harpold 1999: 14) created a prospective profile of a school shooter which included characteristics such as being an isolated white male who dresses sloppily, has a history of mental health treatment, violence, alcohol, and/or drug abuse, and is influenced by "satanic or cult-type belief systems" or violent song lyrics. Similarly, psychologists McGee and DeBernardo (1999) generated their own profile of a classroom avenger as being a socially immature and isolated middle class white male who has no prior history of serious school misbehavior and has been rejected and teased by his peers. Many features of these two widely circulated profiles overlap (especially the focus upon isolated white males), but they also directly contradict one another on numerous points.

While various profiling techniques have gained some measure of empirical support for other types of perpetrators (Homant and Kennedy 1998; Kocsis et al. 2000; Pinizzotto and Finkel 1990), the profiling of young students has proved particularly problematic. Many students who fit general profiles never commit school violence of any kind, while numerous students who have planned and executed attacks at their schools did not match prior profiles (Sewell and Mendelsohn 2000). Such student profiles have recently fallen out of favor, and a systematic investigation of targeted school shooting incidents revealed that there simply "is no accurate or useful 'profile' of students who engaged in targeted school violence" whether demographic, psychological, or social (Vossekuil et al. 2002: 11).

Guided professional judgment and warning signs
Another technique used to appraise students' violence risk is guided professional judgment, which has also been referred to as structured clinical assessment (Reddy et al. 2001). This approach entails evaluation through the use of checklists of risk factors or warning signs for violence (Borum 2000; Otto 2000). Such assessments are sometimes conducted by licensed mental health professionals (Reddy et al. 2001), though school and law enforcement officials have also utilized the various checklists which have been publicized over the years by the Justice and Education Departments (Dwyer et al. 1998), the International Association of Chiefs of Police (1999), and the collaboration between MTV and the American Psychological Association (American Psychological Association 1999). As some of these checklists featured general warning signs such as a "minimal interest in academics," this approach has been criticized for utilizing criteria that are vague and broad enough to apply to the majority of any student body (Fox and Burstein, 2010: 69). While standardized psychological tests and instruments used by mental health professionals have been found to be somewhat accurate in certain contexts with violence in general (Reddy et al. 2001), there is no empirical evidence which suggests that they are successful in predicting targeted school violence with preselected victims (Arluke and Madfis 2014; Borum 2000; Borum et al. 2010).

Automated decision making
Risk assessment approaches classified as automated decision making have been broken into two camps, actuarial formulas and artificial intelligence, both of which "produce a decision...rather than leaving the decision to the person conducting the assessment" (Reddy et al. 2001: 166). The actuarial form of automated decision making is based on purportedly objective algorithms utilizing empirically based criteria which produce outcome scores to determine judgments about the future likelihood of violence (Vincent 2009). Though actuarial measurements have shown some success (Borum 2000), their accuracy is somewhat questionable (Mossman 1994).

Artificial intelligence programs represent the other automated approach to risk assessment. Computer programs render decisions in a manner thought to reduce human error and bias. One such technology developed by a California company for the Bureau of Alcohol, Tobacco, and Firearms, the MOSAIC Threat Assessment System, is frequently used on the campus of Yale University even though it remains extremely controversial (Fox and Burstein 2010; Sachsman 1997). Both types of automated decision making have been criticized for not being sufficiently malleable or flexible (Reddy et al. 2009; Sewell and Mendelsohn 2000; Vincent 2009) and for an inordinate focus upon statistical associations or objective conclusions over complex understandings of causality and etiology (Grubin and Wingate 1996).

The threat assessment approach

The threat assessment perspective is a prolific approach utilized to advance understanding about the causes and manifestations of targeted school violence, a term which refers to "situations in which an identifiable (or potentially identifiable) perpetrator poses (or may pose) a threat of violence to a particular individual or group" (Fein et al. 1995: 1). Initially developed as a "set of investigative and operational techniques that can be used by law enforcement professionals to identify, assess, and manage the risks of targeted violence and its potential perpetrators" (ibid.: 1), the last decade has seen a multitude of school violence research conducted under the threat assessment rubric (Cornell 2003; Cornell et al. 2004; Cornell and Sheras 2006; Deisinger et al. 2008; Fein et al. 2002; Jimerson, Brock, and Cowan 2005; O'Toole 2000; Randazzo et al. 2006; Rappaport and Barrett 2009; Reddy et al. 2001; Strong and Cornell 2008; Twemlow et al. 2002; Vossekuil et al. 2002).

The threat assessment approach differs from previous attempts to discern dangerousness due to its focus upon the substantive analysis of existing threats rather than predicting the future behavior of people based on typical personality profiles, warning signs, or other aggregate data pertaining to individual characteristics. This approach argues that people who perpetrate acts of targeted violence lack a single homogeneous profile, but the evaluation of offenders' backgrounds, personalities, lifestyles, and resources may aid in determining the gravity of threats (O'Toole 2000).

Perhaps most significantly, this perspective asserts that not all threats are equivalent—that is, "there is a distinction between making a threat...and posing a threat...Many people who make threats do not pose a serious risk of harm to a target. Conversely, many who pose a serious risk of harm will not issue direct threats prior to the attack" (Reddy et al. 2001: 168). Critical details, such as how direct, detailed, developed, and actionable the threat is, help to further assess seriousness of the situation. O'Toole (2000) classified threats into four categories: direct, indirect, veiled, and conditional. A direct threat, announced in a plain and unambiguous manner, specifies that a certain action will be taken against a specific target. An indirect threat with tentative phrasing is less clear and definitive. A veiled threat implies but does not overtly intimidate so that there is some question as to how the threat could be interpreted. A conditional threat warns that violence will occur unless certain demands are met. In addition to forming a typology of threats, O'Toole (2000) differentiated between low, medium, and high risk levels. Low-level threats, which pose minimal risk, are vague, implausible, and lack realism. Medium-level threats, which may be carried out but are not wholly realistic, show evidence that the person threatening others has thought through the plan, indicated potential locations and times, but lacks any indication that he/she has taken preparatory steps to act on the threat. Finally, high-level threats, which pose an imminent danger to the safety of others, are direct, detailed, conceivable, and show evidence that concrete steps have been taken toward carrying it out.

Cornell and Sheras (2006) have similarly distinguished between transient and substantive threats. Transient threats are "statements that do not express a lasting intent to harm someone. Transient threats either are intended as figures of speech or reflect feelings that dissipate in a short period when the student thinks about the meaning of what he or she has said" (Cornell and Sheras 2006: 21). In contrast, substantive threats are "statements that express a continuing intent to harm someone...they also indicate a desire to harm someone that extends beyond the immediate incident or argument when the threat was made" (Cornell and Sheras 2006: 22). These scholars further separate substantive threats into serious and very serious threats based on the intended harm to be committed, where a serious threat is a threat to physically assault someone and a very serious threat is to kill, sexually assault, or severely injure someone (Cornell and Sheras 2006).

While violence risk assessment is a diverse and developing field, there are numerous issues and unanswered questions regarding its application in schools around the country. Verlinden et al. (2000: 27) noted that there is a total lack of "data at this point to assist a clinician in selecting the 'best' strategy for risk assessment for violent school assaults." Similarly,

Reddy et al. (2001: 160) pointed out that "[i]t is not currently known how many schools use which type of assessment" and that no data exist which "describe the prevalence of any of these three approaches (or others) schools may currently use, nor of their effectiveness-perceived or actual." Though the pressing need for such knowledge was pointed out more than a decade ago, scholars and practitioners still lack this vital data.

Thus, while the threat assessment approach arguably has attained the most positive evaluations via empirical testing (see Cornell 2013 for a review), the other forms of risk assessment (not to mention the zero tolerance approach that presumes no need for risk assessment at all) may still be preferred or more frequently utilized by school and police officials. Specifically as it relates to this research, nothing is known whatsoever about the role that any of these various risk assessment techniques played during the numerous school rampage attacks which have been averted during the last decade.

Understanding school criminalization and risk assessment as actuarial justice

There has been a dramatic transformation of school discipline and security in American public schools since the turn of the 21st century. Not unlike assertions that contemporary culture represents a post-9/11 era, many school officials refer to a post-Columbine era in public education in which everyone must now think about school safety in an entirely new manner (Muschert et al. 2013). As just discussed, this new way of thinking entails expanded zero tolerance policies that dictate mandatory suspensions, expulsions, and arrests of students, surveillance through the proliferation of police officers and security cameras in schools, and school security which is designed to prevent crime through the environmental design of the school building itself. These developments represent a swift and widespread "penetration of law enforcement personnel and technology into urban, suburban, and rural schools" (Hirshfield and Celinska 2011: 39). Such order-control mechanisms can generally be characterized by a one-size-fits-all approach, as school discipline takes remarkably similar forms in widely divergent school contexts, regardless of whether or not schools have high levels of student misbehavior (Kupchik 2010; Muschert and Madfis 2013).

Though scholars have been describing the changing features of school discipline and security for decades, theoretical insight into the causes of this process has been slower to emerge. Prominent social theorists tackling diverse topics, ranging from the sociology of punishment and education to public policy and legal studies, have addressed the origins and intensification of school criminalization, yet the investigation of this emergent phenomenon has rarely been their sole focus. That said, prominent theoretical insight on larger issues of neoliberalism, punitiveness, and risk has a great deal to contribute to the understanding of the contemporary state of school criminalization and thus warrants extensive discussion.

As the prominent political and legal scholar Bernard Harcourt (2010: 77) has recently stated, neoliberal penality is "today in full fruition." He (ibid.: 77) defines this term as:

> a form of rationality in which the penal sphere is pushed outside political economy and serves the function of a boundary: the penal sanction is marked off from the dominant logic of classical economics as the only space where order is legitimately enforced by the State. On this view, the bulk of human interaction—which consists of economic exchange—is viewed as voluntary, compensated, orderly, and tending toward the common good; the penal sphere is the outer bound, where the government can legitimately interfere, there and there alone.

In many ways, this parallels and augments prior theoretical work on the contemporary culture of control (Garland 2001) and governance through crime (Simon 2006), which emphasize the manner in which anxieties and insecurities regarding all manner of larger structural concerns (about job security, economic prosperity, income inequality, family stability, etc.) are addressed via hardline crime fighting measures. Bell (2011) suggests that a neoliberal form of government, no longer able to attain legitimacy through public services or a social safety net, attempts legitimation through a tough law and order mentality that appeals across class lines (see also Wacquant 2009). This may be aligned with what many have described as the more general penal turn towards a "new punitiveness" which encourages longer sentences and harsher treatment for adult offenders (Pratt et al. 2005).

American public schools have a lengthy tradition of punitive focus upon obedience and discipline (which Brint (1998) attributes to Puritan asceticism and the needs of industrial labor), and the extent to which a new punitiveness has bled into juvenile justice remains a contested topic (Goldson 2002; Muncie 2008; Wald and Losen 2003). However, the criminalized lens through which student discipline is viewed (wherein school misbehavior is transferred to the juvenile and adult justice systems and even childish threats are redefined as terrorist acts) and the securitized lens through which school safety is viewed (wherein schools are made to resemble airports if not prisons) do represent fairly new developments.

Additionally, there is another key aspect to the wider change in penal philosophy that has undoubtedly altered the face of school discipline and security. In his discussion of the transition to a late modern culture of control, Garland (2001: 128) stated that:

> In the past, official criminology has usually viewed crime retrospectively and individually, in order to itemize individual wrongdoing and allocate punishment or treatment. The new criminologies tend to view crime prospectively and in aggregate terms, for the purpose of calculating risk and shaping preventative measures.

Thus, both Garland's (2001: 129) notion of new criminologies and Harcourt's (2010) neoliberal penality are situated within a cultural context wherein society is increasingly concerned with the prediction and alleviation of risk. The modern "risk society" (Beck 1992; Giddens 1999) or "actuarial age" (Harcourt 2007) entails a mindset where there is a preoccupation with the future and the systematic manipulation of risk is achievable, global, and primary.

The administration of justice, in particular, has moved toward an "actuarial justice" mindset that reorients penology toward "techniques for identifying, classifying, and managing groups assorted by levels of dangerousness" (Feeley and Simon 1994: 173). Rather than opting for intervention as a means of retribution or rehabilitation, this so-called "new penology" sees crime as inevitable and seeks instead to manage risk and regulate danger (Feeley and Simon 1992; Rigakos and Hadden 2001). Likewise, Steiker (1998: 774) argues that our justice system increasingly attempts

> to identify and neutralize dangerous individuals before they commit crimes by restricting their liberty in a variety of ways. In pursuing this goal, the state often will expand the functions of the institutions primarily involved in the criminal justice system—namely, the police and the prison. But other analogous institutions, such as the juvenile justice system and the civil commitment process, are also sometimes tools of, to coin another phrase, the "preventive state."

O'Malley (2008) points out that the focus on risk and predictive measures need not be solely punitive, and Garland (2001: 138) notes that a neoliberal view would likely understand "high rates of imprisonment [as] an ineffective waste of scarce resources." However, Harcourt (2010; 2011), through an insightful reading of Foucault's (2009) later work on governmentality, explains how broad trends in neoliberalism relate directly to the transition in governance away from ameliorative forms of preventative treatment (such as anti-poverty programs and mental health facilities) and toward the assessment and management of large numbers of people as dangerous populations in penal institutions.

This punitive and carceral form of prevention and the actuarial mindset that criminal conduct is an unavoidable but manageable risk have certainly expanded into school disciplinary and security practices (Casella 2006; Kupchik and Monahan 2006; Lyons and Drew 2006; Simon 2006). Americans, by and large, exaggerate the prevalence and potential risk of school violence (Aitken 2001; Burns and Crawford 1999; Cornell 2006)—for example, a poll conducted shortly after the 2005 school shooting incident on the Red Lake reservation in Minnesota revealed that nearly three-fourths of Americans believed that a similar attack was "very likely" or "somewhat likely" to happen in their communities (Kiefer 2005). The reality, however, is that "only about 1 in 2,000,000 school-age youth will die from homicide or suicide at school each year" (Muschert 2007: 61) and "any given school can expect to experience a student homicide about once every 6,000 years" (Borum et al. 2010: 27). In the risk society, however, even unfounded and exaggerated perceptions of risk take priority, thus every locale must be wary and implement extensive measures to control risk by preparing for an onslaught of mass violence.

The actuarial justice frame of mind also entails the belief that it is inevitable for certain school students to possess the desire to fatally harm their peers, but the risk of rampage killing may be mitigated through the application of police and prison practices to school settings (i.e. the systematic prediction and surveillance of prospective school shooters and the monitoring and securing of the physical space of school buildings). Therefore it makes sense that, by and large, the response to school rampage as a social problem has been attempts to predict them with risk assessments, punish anything resembling them (such as weapons violations and threatening comments) with harsh zero tolerance policies and transfers to the justice system, deter their occurrence with police officers and cameras, and make them more difficult to accomplish through target hardening procedures like locked doors and metal detectors. This stands in stark contrast to less punitive but more ameliorative and restorative forms of school violence prevention, such as broad-based mental health services, systematic mentoring and support structures, as well as conflict resolution, group conferencing, peer mediation, and anti-bullying school programs (Karp and Breslin 2001; Meyer and Evans 2012; Van Ness and Strong 2010). While the actuarial justice mindset directly informs contemporary school safety, risk assessment, and disciplinary policies, the chapters to follow will illustrate how many of the practices associated with this approach lack empirical evidence indicating their genuine capability to prevent, deter, or predict school rampage violence. This problematic approach frequently presupposes both the inevitability of violence and the flawless nature of deterrence and prediction as currently practiced in American public schools.

2
Assessing the Substance and Risk of Student Rampage Threats

Madfis, Eric. *The Risk of School Rampage: Assessing and Preventing Threats of School Violence.* New York: Palgrave Macmillan, 2014.
DOI: 10.1057/9781137399281.0004.

In the wake of numerous highly publicized multiple-victim shooting sprees which occurred at the close of the 20th century in mostly rural and suburban American public schools, academics, politicians, and media figures weighed in on what should be done to prevent similar events from occurring in the future. One such commentator, Kay Hymowitz, a fellow at the Manhattan Institute, wrote an impassioned essay in favor of emergent zero tolerance policies which automatically mandate strict penalties for student misbehavior such as making threats or bringing weapons to school, regardless of individual or situational circumstances. Hymowitz (2005: 24) stated that such policies:

> have been criticized for resulting in severe penalties for seemingly minor offenses, such as offhand comments about violence, violent drawings, or playful simulations of violent acts. However, the policies have headed off potentially catastrophic shootings and bombings nationwide. Because it is impossible to discern a teenager's true intentions, any hint of potential violence must be taken seriously in order to protect the safety of other students.

Though formed to argue in favor of a policy which has been widely condemned in recent years by various academics (Ayers et al. 2001; Casella 2001; Skiba 2000) and political commentators on both the left (Holcomb and Allen 2009) and right (Schlafly 2003; Whitehead 2001) as well as by the American Bar Association (2001), and the American Psychological Association (APA Zero Tolerance Task Force 2008), her assertion nevertheless directly addresses the difficulty of predicting and responding appropriately to student threats to commit school violence on a massive scale.

Ultimately, zero tolerance approaches evoke an artificial simplicity and certainty to the imminently complicated issue of appraising the violent potentiality of students. Hymowitz (2005: 24) alerts us to this complexity by acknowledging that "it is impossible to discern a teenager's true intentions," yet her insistence that this troubling fact necessarily leads to serious investigations and consequences for violent drawings or rowdy play neglects the impact that such an overzealous school disciplinary environment can have upon the quality, not to mention cost, of American education. Moreover, though she briefly acknowledges the depth of complexity inherent in discerning the true intentions of young people, she ultimately retreats to punitive ideology in the pursuit of the simplicity that zero tolerance claims to provide. While Hymowitz is correct that many school rampage attacks have been averted over the last ten years in the United States (Daniels et al. 2007; O'Toole 2000; Trump n.d.), there is absolutely no empirical evidence of any kind attributing zero tolerance policies to these positive outcomes. As Cornell and Sheras (2006; Cornell 2013) have pointed out, simply excluding students from school via suspensions or expulsions does nothing to resolve the original cause(s) of problems or to prevent conflicts from escalating. In fact, a zero tolerance punishment has the potential to exacerbate the isolation and anger of a student contemplating a rampage attack at their school as various disciplinary infractions have been vital precipitating factors in numerous previous school rampages around the world (Levin and Madfis 2009; Madfis and Levin 2013).

Thus, determining how best to respond to the threatening behavior of students has become an important and controversial task. Some commentators have concluded that schools ought to move beyond the punitive simplicity of zero tolerance discipline and instead adopt an emergent approach that purports to appraise if not predict violent behavior. While this approach takes numerous names in varied disciplines and specializations that pertain to the academic understanding of aggressive behavior, they are often collectively referred to as "violence risk assessment" (Reddy et al. 2001; Andrade 2009). Like the other enhancements of school discipline and security described in the previous chapter (and of which zero tolerance policies constitute one component), the increased value placed upon risk evaluation, control, and management in a post-Columbine actuarial age can similarly explain the major development and popular implementation of risk assessment procedures.

While there have undoubtedly been major advancements in diverse literatures that claim to aid in the contemporary understanding of violent threats and their relationship to violence prediction, the success and underlying consequences of these techniques remain hotly contested (Harcourt 2007; Mossman 2006; Sacco and Larsen 2003) and lacking in extensive empirical testing in the school context (Reddy et al. 2001; Verlinden et al. 2000). In particular, little is known about the manner in which assessments of violence risk are actually understood and conducted by school and police officials, nor how these authorities feel about the evaluative certainty such techniques are designed to provide. The phenomenon of averted school rampage violence represents a crucial arena for the investigation of violence risk assessment in the school context as these incidents, at least in theory, represent the ultimate institutional goal of successful evaluation and intervention during one of the most potentially devastating hazards that schools may face. In addition, knowledge about averted school rampage is surprisingly sparse, and as a result, scholarship is often rife with unexplored and problematic assumptions about what the phenomenon entails and how it may be assessed.

Accordingly, the goals of this chapter are to 1) problematize the notion of averted rampage and clarify what have often been haphazard linguistic distinctions between threat, risk, and plot and 2) examine the forms of evidence present when claims are made that a school rampage threat has been averted. The resultant data prove vital as the phenomenon of averted rampage has yet to be subjected to careful conceptual scrutiny or extensive empirical study. Likewise, it is hoped that the findings and discussion to follow may lead to more sophisticated threat assessment language and guidelines, and subsequently away from both simplistic zero tolerance solutions and problematic predictive and characteristic-based forms of violence risk assessment.

Distinguishing threats, risks, plots, and genuine aversion

As described in further detail in the Methodological Appendix (Chapter 6), the evidence to follow comes from a range of sources—most centrally through the personal accounts of police and school authorities, but I also consulted news reports, police incident reports, legal briefs, and court transcripts from trials and hearings as a way of assuring accuracy via data triangulation. Data are drawn from the in-depth analysis of 11 incidents in which at least some school administrators, police officers, parents, and/or news reporters believed that an incident of school rampage violence was planned but ultimately prevented. As such, the notion of an averted rampage leaves room for a wide range of severity between cases wherein students' genuine desire to complete a rampage attack is problematically assumed. While numerous comments or actions by students have the potential to be classified as evidence of an averted rampage, the application of this uniform label glosses over major differences between cases in terms of the level of premeditated planning, the substance of the threat, and the actual level of risk present (Reddy et al. 2001). Likewise, as the academic study of averted rampage violence is still new and emergent, it is vital to note what a mistake it would be for future researchers to assume too much similarity among the numerous cases described by the media as averted school rampages, plots, risks, and/or threats. The scholarship on violence risk assessment, and the threat assessment literature in particular, help to distinguish between these too-easily-conflated terms and the associated levels of severity that must be recognized if schools are to have an accurate understanding of the extent of the problem of school rampage violence, let alone how to prevent its occurrence or mitigate its risk.

The multi-faceted process by which school and police officials implement these techniques and actually discern the severity of threats in practice warrants far more empirical investigation, and my data reveal the actual criteria utilized in these cases as a means to assess the level of risk. However, before these forms of assessment criteria can be described, it is necessary to problematize the concept of averted school rampage. Beyond the initial operationalization of completed school rampage debated in previous works (such as Newman et al. 2004; Muschert 2007), my data have helped to elucidate the fact that the phenomenon of averted rampage has its own conceptual concerns which must be addressed. Though the terms "threat," "risk," "plot," and "averted" are often used uncritically if not interchangeably by the media and many academics to address the phenomenon, they represent different components of a rampage event and its assessment. Each one of these features warrants specific discussion.

Examining the form and content of threats in averted rampage violence

First, as the threat assessment literature makes clear, one must not conflate the terms threat and risk (Cornell and Sheras 2006; O'Toole 2000). While risks refer broadly to the potential exposure to harm, threats refer more specifically to the declaration of an intention to inflict harm. Thus, threats themselves constitute a major evidentiary factor in the assessment of risk. As some (such as O'Toole 2000; Reddy et al. 2001) have previously noted, not all threats signify serious risk, and some very high risk incidents may likewise take place in the absence of a direct threat—this latter point is often discussed as a problematic feature of the threat assessment approach which is only useful in the presence of an existent threat.

In ten out of the 11 cases under investigation in this study, however, there was evidence of a threat of violence declared against others in some form. The one possible exception, at Greenvale High, entailed a student's list of several of his current and former teachers where the word "fuck" was inserted into the middle of each of the teachers' last names. There is no indication that this handwritten list, found in a notebook in the student's locker, ever would have been shared with anyone else and therefore represented an actual communication of harmful intent, yet it was interpreted as both a threat and hit list by some (though not all) members of school staff. Aside from this particular incident, threats were clearly expressed in the remaining ten cases, and they took at least three distinct forms—via verbal, written, and electronic media.

Verbal threats were the most common. In one occurrence at Finley High School, there were numerous verbal threats. These included: a male student offering to kill, for his female friend, anyone that she didn't like; the same male student telling another girl who drove him to school that he wanted to blow people up at a large public park in the center of the city of Boston; and the same student threatening to cut out the tongue of any of his co-conspirators or other peers aware of the plot, if they were to reveal anything to authorities. In another instance of verbal threatening at Adams High School, a student offered to kill the girlfriend of one of his friends for him, after the friend discussed some issues he was having in their relationship. In addition, in at least five more cases (at Adams, Blane, Courtside, Everton, and Finley), there is evidence that students verbally made mention to various peers of attacking their school, though these comments were often, but not always, perceived as flippant jokes rather than legitimate threats.

This research also revealed numerous electronic threats. In one electronic threat at Adams High School, a student posted YouTube clips of himself shooting a rifle and blowing up pipe bombs which he communicated were "1/8 of the size we're gonna use" and which he sent to at least one other student. In another incident at Hastings Jr/Sr High School, students made death threats on a social networking site against various members of the football team and other popular students. In a similar but much more elaborate electronic threat at Everton High, several students created detailed profiles on a social networking website where they referred to themselves as ES420, the Everton Shooters April 20th.

These online profiles featured a digital countdown clock ticking down to the anniversary of Columbine on April 20th, the Columbine killers listed as heroes, pictures of guns and publically visible communications discussing how serious each member was about the plot, with one comment explicitly stating plans to "kill everyone." In addition to their social network profiles, the students in this case also posted on YouTube three disturbingly violent and threatening videos, one of which shared the same title as a recording made by the Columbine killers called "Hitmen for Hire." Juxtaposed with a series of violent images from Columbine and elsewhere, the students' video montage stated, "Nine years ago two boys has a vision…but they never got to accomplish it…but nine years later two boys will carry out that vision and restore that lost fear into the hearts of millions…comming [sic] this Thanksgiving." While no individuals were directly threatened by name in this latter incident, the video still qualifies as a direct threat in O'Toole's (2000) classification system, for it was expressed in a straightforward manner and identified a specific date and particular albeit symbolic target—the school as a whole.

Several cases also involved written threats. Two cases (at Iverson and Kranston) included deadly warnings written on the walls of boys' bathroom stalls in high school buildings. One such note declared that "Tomorrow will be worse than Virginia Tech," and another one stated that "Columbine could happen here." The other written form of threat was the presence of physical hit lists. These were believed to be present in four of the 11 instances—at Adams, Donovan, Greenvale, and Jefferson. One such hit list consisted of a sheet of paper that was clearly entitled "people to kill," another was labeled "targets" and "social targets," a third list found on students included only the names of several of their peers known to have bullied them, and the fourth one previously mentioned as less clearly a threat consisted of a student listing and cursing the names of several teachers in his notebook.

Examining the levels of risk in averted rampage violence

The actual level of risk for violence present in a given incident of threat is, likewise, not uniform. It is here where the terms risk and threat remain problematically conflated, even in the more nuanced threat assessment literature which first strove to clarify these distinctions. For example, the scholars (Cornell 2013; Cornell and Sheras 2006; O'Toole 2000), who have written what are otherwise arguably the most sophisticated classification schematics for assessing the severity of risk in the presence of existent threats, continue to use the term "threat," as in "high level threats" (O'Toole 2000: 9) and "very serious threats" (Cornell and Sheras 2006: 30), when they are clearly referring to risk, the potential exposure to harm (and thus, the terms "high level risks" and "very serious risks" would be more consistent terminology). This confusing linguistic inconsistency aside, the threat assessment approach of these scholars is very useful in determining the level of risk present in each of the 11 cases.

According to the threat assessment standards laid out by Cornell (2013; Cornell and Sheras 2006), none of the 11 incidents under investigation in this study could be strictly classified as transient threats, those made carelessly in jest or in moments of anger. Six cases (Adams, Blane, Courtside, Donovan, Everton, and Finley) should certainly be classified as very serious substantive threats, as they were death threats with much specificity. These same six cases would also qualify as a "high level of threat," using O'Toole's (2000) classification system, because of the direct, detailed, and plausible nature of their plans and the fact that concrete steps were taken in these cases toward carrying them out.

In contrast, the remaining five cases are less clearly defined for, while they were not momentary acts of anger, they lacked much specificity or any clear indication that the students had taken any steps toward actually carrying them out. They would qualify as either low or medium level threats, according to O'Toole's (2000) system. This is consistent with Cornell's (2013: 381) observation that "threats are a frequent but largely unrecognized occurrence in schools," many of which are not particularly serious. In two of these lower risk incidents (at Greenvale and Jefferson), students who had written lists of the names of people they disliked saw these interpreted as hit lists for rampage shootings. In the Hastings case, students threatened their classmates with violence on a social networking website in a manner that some parents, police, and the media interpreted as genuine and fatal. In the final two incidents (Iverson and Kranston), threats referencing previous school rampage shootings were written on bathroom walls. While the 11 incidents varied widely in severity, at least according to how they would be evaluated via the threat assessment approach, if one was to rely on media coverage alone, it would be rather difficult to discern these very significant differences as all 11 incidents were covered (albeit not to the same extent) as potentially averted rampage plots.

Examining plots and planning in averted rampage violence

The term school "plot," which is often used interchangeably with school rampage in the media, implies a certain amount of previous planning and forethought, but this should more properly be understood as an empirical question. Can there be averted rampage without a plot in place? As the findings section on planning will soon reveal, my data indicate that, while extensive planning represents one of the strongest features to convince officials of students' intentions to do harm, students have been accused, both by their schools and in the press, of being engaged in an averted rampage incident without any indication of the presence of detailed planning. Thus, evidence of a rampage plot, while a very common feature of averted rampages (and likely one of the best indicators of genuine intent), is not a necessary component for some school officials or the news media to label a student's action as an averted rampage incident.

Examining the notion of aversion in rampage violence

Finally, and perhaps most importantly, the term "averted" rampage implies that an attack was inevitably and certainly going to take place before it was prevented. Perhaps, for instance, a student's flippant verbal remarks or written personal grievances could be misinterpreted as genuine threats. Even a carefully planned attack might likewise represent only a hypothetical fantasy for a student who never intended to carry it out. As the findings in this chapter will later indicate, the contentious question of "what would have happened" remains disturbingly unsettled terrain for numerous (though by no means all) school and police officials who have been directly involved in these events. They are often not entirely certain of the genuine intentions of students accused of plotting school rampages, though these officials may increase their certainty through the use of various risk assessment criteria.

The assessment of evidence in averted rampage violence

The categories of evidence utilized as a means to assess the seriousness of rampage violence threats are myriad, but they may essentially be divided into two distinct types. The threat assessment approach emphasizes criteria that signify detailed planning for the crime and active preparations undertaken toward carrying it out. As such, plot details entailing specific people, places, or timing and the training in or existent, potential, or desired access to weapons all represent forms of threat assessment criteria. In contrast, risk assessments based on the identification of individual or group characteristics are more in line with a profiling or warning sign approach. As both types of assessment criteria were either implicitly or explicitly discussed by school and police officials as important for making decisions during the course of handling these cases, they both warrant extensive discussion. These findings will begin with an exploration of the forms of evidence utilized that may be classified as threat assessment criteria (i.e. plot details and the role of weaponry) and then turn to those forms that may be understood as relating to profiles and warning signs of likely school rampage offenders (i.e. individual and group characteristics).

Assessing the plot's detail

The first major category used by school and police officials to determine risk is the level of detail involved in the planning of violence. This criterion is already a vital feature of the threat assessment approach, and, as O'Toole (2000) pointed out, the planning involved in carrying out a school rampage is often a lengthy process. According to Vossekuil et al. (2002), most school rampage shooters create a plan at least two days before initiating their attack on students and/or teachers. Many of them develop and fantasize about their plots for weeks or even months prior to carrying them out (Fox and Levin 1994; Madfis and Levin 2013; Newman et al. 2004; Verlinden et al. 2000; Vossekuil et al. 2002). The Columbine killers, Eric Harris and Dylan Klebold, spent more than a year extensively preparing their attack (Larkin 2007). While it is quite popular to depict mass shootings as the result of individuals simply "snapping" and committing violent onslaughts in a spur-of-the moment manner, this does not accurately describe the vast majority of mass murders, whether they occur on school grounds or elsewhere (Levin and Madfis 2009). In many of the cases under investigation in this study, evidence of planning a school rampage attack was often extensive and constituted a major determinant in the assessment of a threat's severity. For example, Dr. Sable, an adjustment counselor who dealt directly with the students accused of planning a rampage attack at Finley High School noted that, "they spent so much time thinking about the attack that, if it was a fleeting thought, they wouldn't have had maps or this whole list. They also spent so much time coming up with a list of people to harm."

In terms of the physical and digital evidence collected by police and/or school authorities, the existence of detailed plots were determined by the presence of hit lists and even "do not kill" lists, suicide notes, maps of the school with attack plans drawn on them, daily planners and journals describing the desired targets, methods, and outcomes, supply shopping lists, discussions about the plots on social media websites, and internet searches relating to research on how to execute an attack (such as for details about previous rampage shootings, attaining firearms, or building bombs). These various forms of evidence convinced school and police officials that the risk of rampage violence was more significant because of the detailed nature of how the plan was to be strategically implemented. Specifically, plots were comprised of details such as who was to be purposely targeted, what locations were to be attacked in what order, and when the attacks were to take place.

The first subcategory of planning, the extent to which certain individuals or groups were targeted as potential victims, is important not only because school and police officials viewed this as indicative of more serious intent, but because this very issue constitutes a hotly contested debate, both internal and external to academia, about whether or not specific targets are victimized during a rampage attack. Cullen (2009) rather famously argued that prior news accounts misreported the "myth" that the Columbine shooters specifically targeted minorities and jocks (see also Ogle et al. 2003 on the media revisionism of this issue). Likewise, some scholars (Kimmel and Mahler 2003; Volokh 2000) have characterized school rampage shootings as "random" events at least in part because of the much touted (though not empirically tested) notion that school rampage shooters attack peers and teachers in an indiscriminate manner without deliberate targets in mind. In fact, the presence of random victims has often been used as an operational criterion for rampage shootings. For example, Newman et al. (2004) specifically limited her definition of school rampage to include only those cases in which at least some of the victims were chosen randomly or symbolically. Likewise, Muschert (2007) distinguished "targeted" school shootings with multiple specifically intended victims from "rampage" school shootings which necessitate random or symbolic victims. The present study is uniquely suited to tackle this particular question for at least two reasons. First, unlike many of the school rampage killers who have committed suicide (or suicide-by-cop) after completing their deadly plans, my entire sample of would-be school attackers was still alive when they were caught and thus could explain their intentions to police and other officials with whom I was then able to speak. Secondly, in averted incidents, the plots themselves are the criminal offenses and so the extant news media reporting and legal documentation are far more focused on the planning aspects of these cases rather than on other issues more prominently featured in the aftermath of completed rampages, such as offenders' actions on the day of their attacks, the manner in which victims were killed or injured, the victims' identities and extent of their injuries, or the impact of the event upon effected communities, families, and survivors. This wealth of data revealed that most of my sample of cases did in fact desire to target specific individuals or groups of people rather than, or in addition to, random victims and the school as a whole.

In the incident at Adams High School, the people the student planned to kill on the day of his attack were specifically chosen because they were individuals who he felt had slighted him in the past. For example, the sheet of paper found in his bedroom labeled "targets" contained the names of 30 students at the school, as well as the names of four additional students with "NK" (no kill) listed next to their names, and a distinct "Do Not Kill" section listing the names of another 16 students. The student did tell police that his plan was not to kill strangers and only to kill those students who had been picking on him for years. There was also one girl in particular who he wanted to kill, and he had extensive written notes about her, such as where she lived and worked, what vehicle she drove, as well as exactly how he wanted to kill her by shooting her in the head. He also told a friend about wanting to kill her specifically. Further, he informed police that he added the names one by one, gradually over time. However, he also selected what Newman et al. (2004: 50) called "symbolic" targets and what the student, in his notebook, called "social targets." These included various cliques such as "Goths," "Punks," "Commies," "Hippies," "Preps," "Gays," "Ghetto Wiggers," and "Muslims" where asterisks were placed next to the names of certain students to indicate to which groups they belonged. One of his journal entries repeated this theme, as he indicated that he thought many people needed to die, but he singled out "muslims, niggers, spics, towelheads, Goths, punks, and especially faggots."

Many of the other incidents echo this theme. At Courtside High, the would-be rampage killer specifically planned to execute the students he did not like, and even intended to tell his friends at the high school not to attend class on the day of the attack. In fact, this student even convinced one of his friends to hold onto his stolen weapons for him because he promised the friend that he would warn him in advance to assure that he and his girlfriend would not be on the premises. The three Donovan High School students apprehended with an arsenal of weaponry on them also carried a hit list of particular students who had teased them. The Everton High students did target specific people such as the SRO and other administrators, but also discussed attacking people more widely and randomly.

In at least one case, the importance of who was to be targeted was so paramount to the Finley High student plotters that all of the other elements of their planning criteria (such as what locations were to be targeted, when the attacks were to take place, and how the plan was to be strategically implemented) reflected a desire to harm specific people while protecting the safety of others. In this incident, some of the student plotters argued that their group was originally formed to protect kids who were being bullied and only intended to hurt certain individuals. In a binder found at the home of one of the students, police found a hit list with the names of roughly a dozen people on it, including both students and staff. The star football player at the school was a particularly significant target for another member of the group, who felt that this student athlete constantly harassed him. They also intended to kill members of the school administration including the principal and assistant principal, the SRO, and the gym teacher. They harbored special resentment for the gym teacher and desired to torture her by cutting her Achilles tendon, forcing her to run a mile in seven minutes as she had made them do in gym class, and then shooting her in the head if she could not succeed. In addition, they planned to put CO_2 bombs in the lockers of the students that they didn't like. So concerned with seeking revenge upon their targets, they even developed a contingency plan if Plan A, the school rampage attack, didn't work out. Plan B, which they all concluded was far less preferable, was to break into each of their targets' homes to cut their throats. Conversely, they took time to discuss the most strategic way to get all of their friends into the cafeteria in order to protect these certain students from harm. Despite these precautions and the focus on particular targets, the student plotters still desired to kill as many people as possible. They sought to specifically time their attack for 2:02 PM when school was dismissed because they concluded that this was when the highest number of students would be in the hallways.

In three additional cases (Greenvale, Hastings, and Jefferson), threats were made against specific people either online or through written documents which were interpreted as hit lists. In the remaining three cases (Blane, Iverson, and Kranston), it is unclear from all available evidence if those threatened as potential victims would have been randomly selected, targeted as individuals or social groups, or a combination of both. Ultimately, this finding suggests that strict dichotomous distinctions between targeted and rampage violence are at least somewhat untenable. Moreover, whenever specific groups of people or individuals were targeted in the planning process of a rampage plot, school and police officials viewed this as substantially magnifying the risk.

The second subcategory of planning that school and police authorities understood to be a vital risk factor was the extent to which certain locations, both external and internal to the school, were targeted with extensive planning. These plans typically entailed targeting just the school building itself. However, the Donovan High students' goal was to attack the town at large in addition to the school, and, as previously mentioned in the Finely High School case, homicidal home invasions were discussed as a secondary option if a school attack would not be feasible. The Finley High case is also notable here because, in the plan these students devised, they intended first to blow up a gas station on the opposite side of town from the school in order to divert emergency personnel away during the time of their school attack.

Strategic decision making regarding location could also be seen in how some students designated certain areas of the school as targets in their attempt to maximize carnage. In the Adams High case, police found a floor plan map of the school building when they searched the student's bedroom. The map had been extensively written on with lines and arrows to indicate his intended travel routes during the attack and where several propane bombs would be placed. When questioned about this map of the school, he informed the school's SRO that his plan was to start the attack by going to this officer's room in the school and incapacitating him by handcuffing him and taking his radio. He would then proceed to kill his intended targets by starting in the cafeteria and then moving around the building in a counterclockwise circle which would culminate with him committing suicide in the library. In another incident at Everton High, school administrators also found a detailed map of the school, but in this case it was publically available on the website of one of the student plotters, while an additional physical map was found in a student's backpack. These maps had the names of the three students listed on them in different colors, matching color-coded dots and lines going around the building which identified areas within the school that were to be targeted, including the boys' locker room, and the offices of the principal, building security, and the SRO. As in the previous two cases, the students at Finley High also possessed maps of their high school. One was hand drawn and the other was a building floor plan stolen from the SRO's desk. The plan these students devised also included a division of labor so that one student would move to one wing of the school to shoot the jocks where they were in class, while another student killed the SRO, and a third student murdered the administration. Another component of their plan was to put one of them on the roof of the school to kill any approaching emergency personnel who tried to intervene.

A third subcategory of planning was decisions detailing when the attacks were to take place, both in terms of the desired date to execute the rampage and the timing of how the rampage was to proceed on that day. The desired date was frequently the anniversary of the Columbine massacre, which occurred on April 20, 1999. However, in any given year, when April 20th fell on a weekend or during a school vacation, students made do with a date in close proximity. School officials at Adams High found a daily planner in the high school student's locker in which he had highlighted a particular date in April that was the closest school day to April 20th. Likewise, in the case at Finley High, the attack was originally scheduled to take place on April 20th, specifically because of the fact that this was both Hitler's birthday and the anniversary of Columbine, but the date was later changed to April 15th as classes would not be in session on the 20th due to school vacation. However, an April date was not planned in every case. For example, the Everton High students engaged in a detailed conversation on a social networking site about what day should be chosen for their attack. They debated over whether they should choose a random day, the date that Martin Luther King was assassinated, or the first day of school during the following year.

In addition to choosing a specific date for the attack, some students also designed plans for what was to take place in what order on the day itself. The example of this, which occurred at Adams High, was so extreme that Detective Brown, the SRO at the scene when the student's planning folder was discovered, had the following to say about it: "He had it written, verbatim, in chronological order...Exact with detail, step by step. It was wicked wicked detailed. Almost like a briefing that a swat team would have." In fact, the crime/incident report on this case included a copy of what was originally a handwritten document titled "April 10, 2007 NBK Plan" that contained a detailed timeline for the day of the attack. It stated the following:

6:00	1. Wake up at 6:00
6:15	2. Take caffeine pills, energy drinks, and xtra energy etc.
6:40	3. Make sure all guns ammo are ready, bombs are prepped, guns clean, all equipment ready, cigs, lighters, slings, ammo holders, alcohol
7:00	4. Have last meal, place all equipment on side of house
7:15	5. Get dropped off/walk to school
9:30	6. Wait until 9:30 then go back home
10:00	7. Prep, bombs, guns explosive in car
10:15	8. Get cell phone numbers
10:20	9. Enjoy life for half an hour
10:50	10. Go to parking lot, call friends
11:00	11. Prep car bomb, ANFO
11:05	12. Go inside have some fun
	13. When done have some vodka, a smoke
	14. Commit suicide

While other students may have made similarly sophisticated schedules for the day of their attacks (such as at Everton and Finley), only the Adams High School student took the time and care to write it down chronologically moment to moment in such an explicit fashion.

Whether the level of detail present in a rampage plot was found to be about who was to be targeted, where the rampage was to take place, or how and when it would be executed, these specifics were interpreted as signs that threats ought to be considered less improvident or transient. Thus, broadly in line with the threat assessment approach, school and police officials felt that the existence of any and all detailed facets of planning dramatically enhanced the potential risk for violence.

Appraising the role of weaponry

Clearly, the role that weaponry plays in school rampage cannot be overstated. As Levin and Madfis (2009) and Madfis and Levin (2013) note, the availability of and training in firearms are crucial facilitating factors in carrying out a mass murder. Police and school officials consider various aspects of weaponry when they seek to discern if a student has engaged in a plot to commit school rampage. These aspects include the existent, potential, or desired access to weapons, evidence of weapons training, the glorification and fascination with weapons, and threats mentioning the use of weapons.

The first crucial subcategory is the presence of weapons or evidence that students were attempting to attain or manufacture weapons. This criterion has long been cited as crucial in the threat assessment literature in terms of judging how "actionable" a threat may be (Cornell 2013; Cornell and Sheras 2006; O'Toole's 2000), and punishment for students bringing guns to school was the impetus for the initial zero tolerance policies (Ayers et al. 2001; Skiba and Peterson 1999). Though weapons were present in some cases, they were not present in every case nor was there evidence that the accused students sought out or had access to weaponry in all instances. Thus, while weapons possession or access was not viewed as a fundamental necessity in terms of being perceived as a potential rampage incident, it undoubtedly signified increased severity and an enhanced potential for lethal violence to both school and police officials. As Officer Jones, Iverson High's SRO, stated:

> We seriously consider whether he has access to weapons. I always go back and check the in-house computer and see if mom or dad has weapons at home. I've called home and said, "Hi, we're concerned. Are there weapons in the household? Is there access to weapons?" We always find that out. So you take that factor into account, majorly.

Understandably, access to large amounts of lethal weapons represented one of the most significant concerns for school and police authorities.

In the incident at Adams High School, a student amassed a vast arsenal of weaponry including knives, ammunition, two assault rifles, and at least two additional guns all legally registered in his father's name. With his father's permission, the student kept all of these in his bedroom closet. This student had also made numerous pipe bombs in his basement, and many other materials used to manufacture a wide variety of bombs were found in his bedroom. There, police also found a written shopping list of desired supplies that included different firearms, bombs, and bomb-making materials. Another incident at Blane High School involved a student bringing tennis balls to his high school that had been filled with explosives. Police later found four additional explosive devices at the student's home. A third event at Courtside High entailed a student stealing three guns and hundreds of rounds of ammunition from his father's safe before giving them to a friend to hold onto until they would be needed to execute the plot. Yet another case at Donovan High School entailed the arrest of three teenagers who were walking down a street while carrying rifles, handguns, swords, knives, and a shotgun along with thousands of rounds of ammunition, after failing in their attempt to steal a car to embark on a killing spree meant to include the local high school. A fifth incident at Everton High involved numerous students who had taken a large arsenal of weapons, including rifles, shotguns, and handguns, from their parents' collections. On a social networking website, they discussed the need to attain earplugs to protect their hearing while firing the weapons.

Unlike the previous five cases, in the incident at Finley High School, none of the four student plotters were found with firearms or explosives, but they were stockpiling gunpowder and had previously created and tested many homemade explosives including napalm. According to a shopping list found in the bedroom of one of the boys, they were also actively attempting to attain trip wire explosives, cannon fuses, PVC piping, semi-automatic weaponry, propane tanks, as well as chains and bike locks to seal the rear and main doors of the school. One of the accused plotters approached at least two other students on separate occasions to request that firearms be purchased or lent out to him, but he was denied in both attempts. This same student also indicated that he could access guns by stealing them from his father who was a police officer. In each of the aforementioned four cases where juveniles gained access to firearms, these weapons were legally registered in their parents' names. In all of the six cases listed above, a large portion of school and police officials expressed serious concerns about students' intentions which were directly linked to their access to weapons. In contrast, in the remaining five incidents (Greenvale, Hastings, Iverson, Jefferson, and Kranston), there was no evidentiary or even speculative indication of the presence of any weapons of any kind, nor the attempt on the part of the plotters to attain weapons, and confidence that students intended to carry out their threats was far less uniform in these cases.

Another major criterion noted by school and police officials was evidence that students had actively been training with weapons for their attack (no officials indicated the presence or importance of any other form of training such as physical training, though firearms and explosives surely make mass murder easier to accomplish in the absence of physical fitness). Though even the Columbine shooters videotaped footage of themselves engaged in target practice in the foothills near their homes, weapons training has not previously emerged or been addressed in any of the risk assessment literature. Evidence of training with weapons included physical remnants or damages left after the activity took place or any account or documentation that such preparation occurred. In only two of the cases under investigation did officials confirm that students actively trained with weapons for a school rampage assault, but the training evident in both of these cases was abundant. In the averted incident at Adams High, a student admitted to making over 40 pipe bombs over a four year period, including CO_2 bombs, copper pipe bombs, dry ice bombs, and cherry bombs. One of his bomb-making friends put the number closer to one hundred bombs over a two year period. The student also filmed himself on numerous occasions blowing up his homemade bombs along with footage of himself firing his father's guns at a shooting range to improve his aim. After being informed about his frequent training sessions in the woods near his parent's home, police searching this area found the remnants of numerous explosive devices. The other plot (at Finley High) which involved extensive training for a school attack similarly entailed a great deal of time devoted to weapons preparation. In this instance, the students also admitted that they spent time in a deserted wooded area where they did target practice and blew up homemade explosives. They experimented by blowing up gun powder in various containers, and even made napalm by thickening gasoline with Styrofoam and lighting it on fire. Though these students, despite their best efforts, were never able to attain their own firearms, they did acquire BB guns, knives, and axes, all of which they practiced shooting and throwing at trees which they pretended were their intended victims. Police searching these woods found cans and bottles that had been exploded as well as large gashes in the trees of the surrounding area.

In both of these cases, the intensity of weapon preparation and training was extensive. While an interest in firearms may be a fairly common trait among American adolescent boys (Shapiro et al. 1997), the level of experimentation and fascination present in these two incidents is certainly out of the norm of typical youth behavior, and rightly concerned the school and police officials who learned about these activities. Therefore, the notion of training may be appropriately considered a new addition to the threat assessment literature, and one which certainly qualifies as the sort of concrete step taken toward carrying out an attack which O'Toole (2000) described as indicative of high level threats.

In contrast, though school and police officials certainly noted that the student plotters in several of these incidents demonstrated a longstanding fascination with weaponry such as firearms and explosives, the broad interest in weapons more generally did not constitute a vital indicator in their assessments. Despite the fact that a fascination with weapons has been described as a warning sign for school shootings going back to some of the earliest research (Band and Harpold 1999; Leary et al. 2003; McGee and DeBernardo 1999), the officials' seeming lack of concern here might reflect the adoption of the more nuanced threat assessment evaluative mindset over an emphasis on warning signs and profiles which may apply to a broad swath of the population. In other words, a student's interest in weapons (which may be a potential warning sign for school rampage but also applies to many adolescents who would never dream of committing such a crime) didn't represent a significant concern for school and police authorities unless their access to or desire for weapons occurred in the context of an existent threat.

This more nuanced approach to assessing violence risk played out in one incident (at Everton High) where several school administrators and the SRO were monitoring the social networking sites of some of their students about whom they were concerned because the students had posted numerous references praising the Columbine massacre in great detail. The school staff did not collectively make the determination to intervene until they saw a picture of a gun posted as the wallpaper on one of the student's websites along with a conditional threat referencing a firearm that stated, "I swear to god. One more mother fucker says the wrong fucking thing to me and I will pull out a goddamn 45 and kill their sorry asses." Mr. Dougherty, one of the house principals at the school, clarified that at that crucial point in time, "We said, 'All right. Now we've got a mention of a 45. We've got an actual mention.' And Trooper Smith [the SRO] said, 'Okay, now is the time to do something about this.'" Thus, the threat referencing a gun combined with the firearm imagery used as wallpaper represented the decisive criteria in this incident. Similarly, at Adams High, it was a threat to utilize bombs communicated electronically that ultimately initiated serious investigation into the student's activities and already well-known enthrallment with firearms and explosives.

Ultimately, while the existent, potential, or desired access to weapons and evidence of weapons training represented significant assessment criteria for school and police authorities (i.e. a sufficient cause for concern), it was not a necessary condition to be judged an averted rampage attack as several incidents did not involve evidence of weapons in any way. Likewise, though a fascination with weapons amplified concern in the presence of an existent threat alluding to their use, an interest in weapons did not by itself foster great concern among school authorities.

Assessing the role of personal and group characteristics

In addition to the significance of weaponry and detailed planning, various personal and group characteristics were often considered as a component of the assessment process. Unlike the previous two evaluative categories which are more in line with a threat assessment approach, concern with individual characteristics and personality traits is more closely aligned with the profiling and guided professional judgment (warning sign) approach to violence risk assessment. Within this grouping of criteria, individual characteristics (such as ethnic/racial and gender identity as well as previous behavior and mental health concerns) and social characteristics (such as school social status and an affiliation with the culture of deviant groups) both represented significant evaluative factors for police and school officials as part of stereotypical school shooter profiles or warning signs.

Both of the original school shooter profiles (Band and Harpold 1999; McGee and DeBernardo 1999) described typical offenders as white males. In fact, mass murder, of which school rampage violence constitutes a subset, is the only form of homicide that is committed by non-Hispanic whites in numbers disproportionately high relative to their share of the population (Fox and Levin 1998: 435; Madfis 2014b). While it is certainly not the case that all school rampages have been committed by whites (for example, the Red Lake Senior High School killer was Native American, the Virginia Tech shooter was Korean American, and the shooter at the Tasso da Silveira Municipal School was Brazilian), the vast majority have in fact been white. As a result, some (Schiele and Stewart 2001; Madfis 2014b; Wise 2001) have attempted to theoretically link white racial identity and privilege to rampage. Additionally, many researchers (Collier 1998; Consalvo 2003; Kimmel and Mahler 2003; Klein 2005; Mai and Alpert 2000; Neroni 2000; Schiele and Stewart 2001) have observed that the vast majority of rampage school shooters have been male (in fact, Latina Williams of Louisiana Technical College is the only female multiple-victim school shooter in American history who was a current or former student of the school she attacked) and asserted the role that dominant notions of masculinity play in reinforcing and legitimizing such violence.

Despite these myriad academic studies asserting the significance of demographic variables, none of my respondents would acknowledge that race/ethnicity or sex/gender played any role in how schools or the police assessed risk. This omission may simply reflect social desirability bias on the part of respondents wary that the use of any such criteria would be interpreted as prejudicial. However, as African American youth are vastly overrepresented in school suspensions and expulsions when compared to white students who commit identical infractions (Fenning and Rose 2007; Robbins 2005), the adjudication of school discipline is anything but colorblind and profiling based on whiteness would go markedly against the grain.

In contrast, maleness has long been associated with increased rates of offending and arrest for violence and delinquency (Messerschmidt 1993), and so it would have been less surprising to hear some respondents acknowledge that they might, for example, be more suspicious upon hearing rumors of a rampage plot hatched by male students than by female students. This was not the case as nearly all of my respondents, regardless of whether they were school administrators, police officers, teachers, or counselors, emphatically stated that gender was not something they take into consideration in making assessments about the risk for student violence. In one of the more frank statements in this regard, the vice principal at Courtside High, Mr. O'Brien, stated, "It doesn't matter if it's a boy or girl, I've seen some girls do serious damage." In fact, most respondents reacted to questions pertaining to gender by dismissing its significance entirely and recounting personal experiences dealing with violent female students. For example, when asked whether he would assess the homicidal threats made by both boys and girls in the identical manner, Dr. Phelps, a school psychologist at Greenvale, responded affirmatively that:

> Oh absolutely, yes. Girls sometimes are significantly violent. We had a situation at the high school... There were two sisters, I think one was grade nine and the other one may have been grade eleven. They took on two security people and four police department people trying to get them off the bus.

I mean they could be tough. We're not gender specific. We're more tuned into the degree of threat.

Stories that discounted the role of gender by alluding to female violence were common. Not only do such tales amount to discounting aggregate patterns through idiosyncratic examples, but they blur the distinction between fairly typical assaults, which girls may commit with some frequency, and multiple homicides, which are, by and large, committed almost exclusively by boys and men (Fox and Levin 2011; Madfis 2014b).

Interestingly, of the 23 students[1] accused of being involved with planning a rampage attack at the 11 schools under investigation in this study, only one was a female. Notably, this girl was accused in the case at Jefferson Middle School, which was previously discussed as a low to medium level threat without any indication of an existent, potential, or desired access to weapons and little evidence of detailed planning outside of having written a list of people she disliked on a sheet of paper that her teacher discovered. The principal of her middle school, Mr. Anderson, did take this girl's gender into account regarding her ultimate lack of genuine intent as he ascribed the girl's motivation for writing the list in the following manner:

> It was because of all the stuff that we see in middle school, especially with girls. It's the jealousy. It's the cliques, okay... The girl who wrote this list, she just was mad at people. That's all. She was mad at these kids. Maybe somebody stole a boyfriend. Maybe they didn't want to be her friend, and she wanted to be their friend. And so she was frustrated and she wrote it on paper and that was as far as it was ever going to go, in my determination, 99.9 percent, you know.

Thus, while nearly all respondents dismissed the role of male gender as a relevant factor both in theory (i.e. that any connection could be found between masculinity and rampage) and in practice (as gender was not deemed germane in the ten incidents involving male students), gender became a suitable mitigating factor for the girl's behavior in her case. This inconsistency becomes particularly distinct when one considers that the same descriptors which were used to mitigate this girl's actions (frustration with peer cliques and relationship troubles) have been used by many scholars to help explain the actions of male school shooters (for example, see Burgess et al. 2006; Kimmel and Mahler 2003; Klein 2005; 2006a, b; Larkin 2007; Leary et al. 2003; Levin and Madfis 2009; Meloy et al. 2001; Newman et al. 2004). That said, and notwithstanding the lack of additional evidence in the Jefferson Middle School case which likely suggests that this girl did not genuinely intend to cause harm, Mr. Anderson is entirely correct, in probabilistic terms, to view her gender as indicative of decreased risk for committing a school rampage. What's more, the unwillingness, or at least hesitation, on the part of respondents to consider gender as a relevant factor in cases with accused male students may reflect larger patterns of privilege where male (just like white) operates as the default, thus rendering the discussion of gender only pertinent to females (Irigaray 1985).

Another element of personal characteristics frequently considered was the previous misbehavior of accused students. One school administrator, Dr. Warner, stated that, "the best predictor of violence is past aggression and violence. That's unequivocal." While this may be the case for violence in general (Campbell 1991; Campbell et al. 1986; Farrington 1991; Moeller 2001; Robins 1966), the same cannot necessarily be said for perpetrators of school violence. In their study of school shooters, Verlinden and his colleagues (2000) found that nine out of the ten students under investigation had some history of aggression and seven out of ten had a history of discipline problems. However, a report commissioned by the U.S. Secret Service and the U.S. Department of Education (Vossekuil et al. 2002: 22) on incidents of targeted school violence (a broader category than that of Verlinden et al. 2000) found that just 13% of their sample of "attackers were known to have acted violently toward others at some point prior to the incident." Similarly, Vossekuil et al. (2002: 20–22) found that only 27% had any prior arrest history, another 27% of the offending students had ever been suspended, only 10% had been expelled at some previous point in their lives, and 63% had never been or were rarely in trouble at school.

Prior histories of aggression and school discipline, and the lack thereof, were, however, often brought up as influential factors in the assessment of risk. For example, the principal, adjustment counselor, and SRO directly involved in the case at Finley High each noted the prior troubling behavior of at least one of the accused students. In addition, the police officer who arrested these students made it clear that he already knew three out of four of them as they "had a history" with the town police department.

In the same way, during the numerous instances when the accused students had no prior behavioral issues, school and police officials expressed doubt regarding the authenticity of the risk. For example,

Mr. Dougherty, a house principal at Everton High, recalled that "none of these kids had a discipline record or anything." Similarly, the assistant principal of Courtside High School, Mr. O'Brien, pointed out that when a parent came to express concern over the deadly intentions of one of his son's friends, he originally discounted the risk because that student had not been in trouble previously. He stated:

> I remember thinking, well, whatever, I've never seen this kid for any type of discipline before that I can remember that was a major problem or issue. Both of these students really were not what you would call major behavior problems. I did not even know who these two students were until this whole incident started to unravel.

Therefore, though having a history of aggression and school misbehavior may not be unequivocally linked empirically to school rampage, school and police authorities certainly valued this criteria, whether that meant giving students they had not previously come across in a disciplinary setting the benefit of the doubt, assuming students they did have prior positive relationships with would be less likely to plot a violent act, or deeming past misbehavior indicative of enhanced risk for violence.

The next factor that school and police officials weighed in their assessments of personal characteristics was the mental health issues of accused students which were often perceived to be indicative of a troubled mind and increased likelihood of violence risk. Subsumed under this category were formal mental health diagnoses, but also comments, notes, or drawings revealing suicidal or depressed thoughts. Many of these criteria have already been subjected to extensive empirical testing. In their investigation of 16 cases, McGee and DeBernardo (1999: 11) included severe mental illness, such as schizophrenia and bi-polar disorder, as "characteristics NOT associated with classroom avengers." Similarly, Vossekuil and his colleagues (2002: 21–22) found that just over a third (34%) of student attackers in their study had received a mental health evaluation during their life, and less than a fifth (17%) had been diagnosed with a mental health or behavior disorder prior to the attack. However, this study also indicated that 78% of attackers exhibited a history of suicide attempts or suicidal thoughts at some point before their attack and 61% had a documented history of feeling extremely depressed or desperate. Likewise, in their sample of ten rampage school shooters, Verlinden et al. (2000: 43) found that only two of them had previously experienced mental health treatment, but eight out of ten exhibited signs of depression, six had made suicidal threats, and another six had created violent writings or drawings.

While mental health concerns such as depression, personality disorders, and psychoses were discussed as a key hypothetical cause of rampage school shootings by a large portion of respondents, evidence of these mental health concerns was rarely abundant in these cases. However, any indication that students were of poor mental health was taken very seriously and seen as a profoundly significant warning sign for violence. For example, only in the case at Finley High was there an accused student with a documented history of being institutionalized for mental illness, which occurred after the student was thought to be a suicide risk—though some school officials incorrectly believed he had been institutionalized for threatening his mother with a knife. This troubled history was discussed by everyone interviewed about the incident and was brought up during legal proceedings, thus it surely played a significant role in how both risk and intent were assessed in this case.

Likewise, school and police officials weighed heavily evidence of depression or suicidal thoughts, though these were existent in the minority of incidents (only in the cases at Adams, Courtside, and Finley). Thus, the school principal at Courtside High, Mr. Fernandez, explicitly noted the vital role that he thought depression, if not suicidal thinking, played in motivating the student's threat which enhanced his concern. Mr. Fernandez said:

> I started talking to around 10–15 students that were in class with the student who had [been accused of stealing his father's gun] and I kind of got the same picture, basically that he doesn't have any friends, maybe one friend, they said. He doesn't talk in class. He doesn't participate in class. They don't really think he has any hobbies or that he's into anything... He just presented as someone who was kind of down in the dumps, anxious and I don't know if you'd say suicidal, but he just looked like he was in pain when I was talking to him. He just didn't look like he was feeling well.

The presence of suicidal thoughts or comments, more generally, was cause for concern. When Detective Brown, Adams High's SRO, initially questioned the accused student in that case, the student admitted to being suicidal, and this did factor into the officer's ultimate conclusion about intent. Police later discovered in the student's bedroom two typed suicide notes. One of these was a detailed note for his parents and the other was intended for everyone else and addressed to a few of his friends. According to the police incident report, the student stated in the second letter that:

> I want to commit suicide, but I don't want all of you to be heartbroken, so to make it easier for you all by shooting up the school, that way you all would hate me, and I won't worry about anybody missing me. Except my family... I would save everyone's grief by committing suicide but I figured I would rather have some fun and revenge and then kill myself.

Commenting upon the existence of these notes, Detective Brown stated, "That kind of clinched it."

Similarly, Courtside Assistant Principal O'Brien discussed becoming increasingly distressed about the student under suspicion when he spoke with the student's English teacher who recalled finding a particular assignment strange and disturbing. According to Mr. O'Brien, the drawing was "a picture of a tombstone and it said rest in peace and it had [the student's] name and it had some year in the future." Yet another of the student's drawings depicted a person being shot along with the words, "I wish this was me. I hate my life." Thus, in addition to documented mental health concerns, comments, notes, or drawings that reflected depression or suicidal ideation drew a great deal of attention from school and police officials, as they represented stark indicators of concern if not culpability.

In addition to the role of individual identity characteristics, school and police officials also considered group dynamics and membership affiliations. The first criterion deemed relevant was social status at the school. Being marginalized by and socially isolated from the rest of the school community are traits long associated with school shooter profiles and warning signs (Band and Harpold 1999; Dwyer et al. 1998; McGee and DeBernardo 1999), but subsequent empirical scholarship has provided mixed results. Though some scholars (such as Langman 2009ab; O'Toole 2000; Vossekuil et al. 2002) have rejected the characterization of all rampage school shooters as "loners," much case study research has found plentiful evidence of isolation and marginalization (for example, Lieberman 2008; Madfis and Levin 2013; Meloy et al. 2004; Newman et al. 2004; Newman and Fox 2009). A careful reading across these studies indicates that the characterization of school rampage offenders as significantly marginalized if not entirely isolated is accurate for a large portion, though by no means all, of previous offenders.

The view that social marginalization and peer group conflict plays a considerable role in causing school rampage violence was common among the vast majority of my respondents who often described accused students as "isolated," "unpopular," "socially different," "unconnected," or "on the periphery." For instance, Finley High School principal, Mr. McGowan, explained his general belief in how social marginalization plays a role in leading to extreme violence. He said:

> I think when you look at all of the school violence issues that have happened, usually it's a kid that for some reason hasn't been able to make or create positive relationships in school. And so, they pull back, and they spend more time either introverted in the internet world, or they pull back and they find a small group of people that are all of the same likeness and then they start talking about, "Why are we the outcasts? Why aren't we part, you know?" So I think there's a pretty clear picture as to the understanding of who those kids are.

The significance of social marginalization as a predictor for school rampage was not only alluded to in the abstract by the school officials involved in this incident. Finley High's adjustment counselor, Dr. Sable, recounted witnessing some of the students who would later be accused of planning an attack on the school being mistreated by their peers at a school-sponsored gathering. She recalled that:

> Those two kids just didn't seem to fit. They fit with each other, and they don't seem to fit anywhere else. Those two kids were trying to dance and be with another group of kids, and the kids just kind of kept turning their back to them and turning their back to them and just leaving them out. Whether the kids truly understood what they were doing, they just kept shutting these two boys out, just shut them down, just kept, you know, with their body language, just kind of kept pushing them out on the periphery... And you know this is a leadership camp where these kids are expected to be leaders and this is how they're treating other kids and it was very telling.

Dr. Sable described witnessing this episode as "a turning point" for both herself and the principal, and she reflected that "as we look back, we were both thinking that it was interesting that we would sit there and take that all in, watch it all unfold, and then have that huge thing happen." Thus, for both Mr. McGowan and Dr. Sable, there was a direct link between how the students were treated by their peers and their creation of a rampage plot, and their witnessing of this event certainly impacted how they later assessed the seriousness of the threat.

Though this view was dominant, it did not amount to universal consensus. For example, Dr. England, Blane High's school psychologist, diminished the role of school social status and peer group conflict as a cause of rampage. She stated:

> When you think of Columbine, you think, you know, the jocks and then these guys who felt really put down by them, and so forth. But that happens with a lot of cliques who are part of high school culture, so I certainly wouldn't just put the blame on that. I mean I think there are much more deeper issues for those students...really mental illness.

Dr. England makes a valid point that social marginalization and bullying are widespread features of school life, and this cannot, by itself, explain rare instances of rampage. It can be, however, one crucial component in a larger multi-causal nexus (Muschert and Ragnedda 2010; Henry 2009; Levin and Madfis 2009; Madfis and Levin 2013; Newman et al. 2004), and thus it is understandable that so many school and police officials view marginalized social status as an important assessment criterion.

Directly related to the notion of social marginalization, the other important criterion based on group characteristics was an affiliation with the culture of deviant groups. In numerous instances, such affiliations, particularly the music and clothing styles associated with certain subcultures such as neo-Nazi skinheads and Goths, were mentioned as informing perceptions about intent. This may be routed in much of the initial reaction to Columbine when musician Marilyn Manson and the Gothic subculture (through associated attire like black trench coats) were blamed for inspiring the attack (Muzzatti 2004; Ogle et al. 2003) and many scholars explored the role played by warning signs such as a "preoccupation with violent media/music" (Verlinden et al. 2000: 43) or "some interest in violence, through movies, video games, books, and other media" (Vossekuil et al. 2002: 22).

In the incident at Donovan High, an assistant principal pointed out that all three of the students involved in the incident often wore black trench coats, and were teased by much of the student body for doing so. In two additional cases (at Adams and Finley), school administrators, police officers, and legal documentation about the incidents all made specific mention about the accused students wearing black trench coats. While one must be careful about forming broad causal links between any item of clothing worn by lots of innocent people and rare instances of extreme violence, there may be some level of legitimacy in linking trench coats with school shootings in that this particular item of clothing has become widely associated with the Columbine killers who did wear them. As the vast majority of rampage plotters around the world since the 1999 Columbine massacre have been directly inspired by that attack (Larkin 2009; Madfis and Levin 2013), signs that students want to repeat elements of Columbine warrant concern. In particular, there are times when clothing choices may genuinely warrant additional suspicion and scrutiny. For example, one of the students accused of plotting a school rampage at Finley High once wore a t-shirt to school which featured a picture of the Columbine shooters on it above the words "Remember the Heroes." This student also reportedly wore swastika t-shirts and drew Nazi symbols on his body in marker. In a separate incident at Adams High School, whereupon, after having police find a black trench coat, a white Jason (from the *Friday the 13th* horror films) mask, and camouflage cargo pants in his bedroom closet, the student proceeded to inform them of his intent to wear these items on the day he would have attacked the school. Police also found, inside a folder full of other planning materials, a hand drawn image of the student dressed in this trench coat, pants, and mask, while armed with shotgun shells, pipe bombs, magazines, Molotov cocktails, knives, and a duffel bag with bombs. All of these items were labeled individually in the drawing. According to one of the police officers who arrested him, the student additionally commented that he specifically chose the pants and coat in order to hold the maximum amount of pipe bombs.

Certainly, Nazi imagery and specific allusions to Columbine or other school rampages should raise red flags for concerned parents and educators, but these were not the only clothing features that emerged in discussions with police and school officials. In numerous incidents, authorities asserted the significance of certain alternative styles, such as black Gothic attire, tattoos, and the shaved heads and suspenders associated with the skinhead subculture. For example, Ms. Grey, a former teacher of a student accused with writing threatening notes on Iverson High School's bathroom walls, shared her view that:

> If you see people walking around in trench coats, hats down over their eyes, drawing weird pictures or covered in, I mean I suppose it's politically incorrect, but covered in tattoos or whatever, pay attention, do something.

Though youth subcultures are perennially blamed for a myriad of social ills, it is vital to reiterate the fact that both the skinhead (in both its anti-racist and neo-Nazi incarnations) and Gothic subcultures have had long histories before the contemporary era of school rampage violence (Haenfler 2009). Additionally, it is extremely problematic to form broad associations declaring common subcultural stylistic choices such as black clothing and tattoos to be signifiers of delinquency, let alone indicators of the next potential school shooter (Muzzatti 2004). Not only does the focus on these cultural preferences have the potential to marginalize a large segment of students who have done nothing wrong other than to subscribe to less traditional beliefs, values, and/or aesthetics, but it is a flawed guideline with little empirical basis. Numerous students who have attempted and completed school rampage shootings have dressed in a traditional manner. In fact, the official *Columbine Report* by the Jefferson County Sheriff's Office eventually debunked the notion that even Harris and Klebold "regularly cloak[ed] themselves in symbols associated with violence or the Goth culture; rather, they 'appeared outwardly normal, [sharing] their dark side only with each other'" (Ogle et al. 2003: 23). What's more, the Adams High School student plotter wanted to deliberately target Goths as victims, and the rampage plot by student athletes at Courtside High was taken less seriously by school officials, at least preliminarily, as a result of their clean cut appearance.

In contrast, perhaps it should be evidence of an abnormal fascination with rampage violence which should stand out as the disconcerting warning sign. In many cases, evidence indicating just this sort of deep and consuming obsession with the Columbine case and other school rampages did exist (in the form of internet searches, comments to peers, and personal writings) and was noted as a decisive factor for both school and police officials. In this criterion, the presence of the copycat effect, where various features of a highly publicized crime are imitated by others (Coleman 2004), was not lost on the officials assessing these cases. For example, a house principal at Everton High, Mr. Dougherty, reflected upon how his concern was exacerbated when he found out from several of the peers of one of the accused students that he "was almost obsessed with Columbine and that he literally...would sit in the cafeteria, and he would ask kids to quiz him on Columbine, like ask him any fact about it." Police and school officials involved in the case at Adams High pointed out computer records revealing that the student had extensively researched Columbine and numerous other mass shooting events. In this student's bedroom, police also found a red folder with a picture of Columbine killers, Eric Harris and Dylan Klebold, on the cover. In multiple journal entries, he referred to his plan to attack the school as "NBK," the same code name (referencing the film *Natural Born Killers*) used by Harris and Klebold. The Finley High students, like in the case at Adams High, had also been referring to themselves as the Natural Born Killers. Officer Dudley, Finley's SRO, described the accused teenagers as being "fascinated with Columbine" and noted that, when one of the student's computer was seized, it indicated that someone had been extensively researching the details about Columbine, as well as material on firearms and bomb making.

By and large, evidence of the copycat phenomenon and a clear obsession with the minutia of previous school rampages did produce greater concern among the respondents than affiliations with youth subcultures such as violent media or subcultural attire, but the latter more problematic associations were still present in the views of some respondents. As such, it's important to recognize this particular assessment criteria for what it is, bias against students with less traditional beliefs, values, and/ or aesthetics, and as such, caution against the practice in future empirical research and risk assessment practices.

Conclusion

The phenomenon of averted school rampage presents several unique dilemmas distinct from those of completed school rampages. In these cases, violent schemes and threats have the potential to be either exaggerated or dismissed. Various forms of violence risk assessment provide guidance to school and police officials in how they evaluate the substance of threats—these range from assessing the detail of plots, appraising the role of weaponry, and numerous criteria based on characteristics like ethnic/racial and gender identity, previous disciplinary and mental health history, school social status, and affiliation with deviant groups.

This chapter explored the myriad forms of evidence utilized to assess the seriousness of student threats and discussed the empirical support, or lack thereof, for these evaluative criteria. Risk assessments based upon the identification of characteristics, regardless of whether they are at the individual or group level, remain a contentious area of debate for scholars. Though research has demonstrated that some descriptive traits (i.e. gender and marginalization) have more reliable empirical backing than others (such as race/ethnicity and histories of behavior problems and mental illness), these distinctions are not widely understood or acknowledged by police officers, teachers, administrators, counselors, or even many scholars of school violence. Consequently, problematic forms of risk assessment are still broadly considered in the decision making processes of school and police officials.

That said, school and police officials do not understand all forms of risk assessment to be equally valid and do privilege certain types of evidence. The next chapter investigates precisely this distinction and addresses the evidence and specific circumstances which lead officials to express confidence in the methods of risk assessment and to believe that justice was carried out properly.

Note

1   One student was accused in the cases at Adams, Blane, Greenvale, Iverson, Jefferson, and Kranston, two students at Courtside, three students at Donovan and Everton, four students at Finley, and five students at Hastings.

3
Confidence and Doubts about Assessing Averted Rampage Violence

Madfis, Eric. *The Risk of School Rampage: Assessing and Preventing Threats of School Violence.* New York: Palgrave Macmillan, 2014.
DOI: 10.1057/9781137399281.0005.

In the study of averted incidents of school rampage, one of the most pertinent questions that must be addressed is whether or not the accused students actually intended to carry out their homicidal plans. No one but the perpetrators themselves can possess complete certainly about this vital question, though various forms of risk and threat assessment may provide insight.

The forms of evidence discussed in the previous chapter that were utilized to assess the seriousness of student threats were significant factors not only for the administration of justice to proceed (i.e. the adjudication of offenders in school and/or court). These criteria were also vital in determining how school and police officials make sense of what is otherwise a rather confusing and uncertain experience with what ultimately amounts to a hypothetical event. This chapter explores how school and police officials interpret the magnitude of evidence in their assessments of the likelihood of a potential rampage. Understanding how school and police officials manage and sometimes fail to come to terms with deciphering whether or not homicidal plots would actually have been carried out may lead to a more realistic expectation of what the practice of violence risk assessment can ultimately strive to achieve—namely, the targeting of at-risk youth for additional preventative measures rather than punitive zero tolerance punishment across the board, and the punishment of people for the crimes they have committed rather than maintaining unrealistic and unfounded expectations about our abilities to predict students' future violent behavior.

Variations in confidence and doubt by risk assessment type

While all types of school and police officials (administrators, security and police officers, teachers, and counselors) interviewed in this study made use of some forms of risk assessment in coming to conclusions about students' intent, there was some variation by job type. Broadly it did appear that police and security officers were most convinced by indications of detailed planning and weapons acquisition, while counselors were the most reliant upon the use of identifying characteristics. Administrators and teachers fell somewhere in the middle, though they often saw the most value in knowing students' personal and behavioral histories. My data, being qualitative in nature with a small sample that was not randomly selected, cannot assert generalizable relationships between occupations and assessment preferences, and so this finding is, at best, preliminary and tentative.

In comparison, the detailed knowledge gleaned from qualitative exploration into these cases with numerous officials tasked with assessing and intervening in them does facilitate important comparisons regarding how officials interpret the varied forms of evidence. The utilization of various forms of risk assessment criteria (such as detailed and developed plans, the existent, potential, or desired access to weapons, and conformity to stereotypical school rampage shooter profile characteristics) certainly did enhance how confident people were about their students' ultimate intentions. The threat assessment criteria are notable for providing people with the greatest amount of certainty, far above and beyond that of identifying characteristics. However, this was not always the case and the recognition of other additional factors, such as different motives and shows of remorse, gave officials doubts about whether students genuinely intended to go through with the attacks they were accused of plotting.

Certainty based on a convergence of risk assessment criteria

Ideally, at least from a risk assessment approach, the more of the aforementioned types of detailed planning, weapons acquisition, and conformity to profile characteristics that were evident in particular cases, the more confident officials would be of the students' genuine intentions to execute their deadly thoughts. Broadly, this was the case, as many school and police officials could utilize the above risk assessment criteria in order to assure themselves of the inevitability of students' actions. Thus, the numerous forms of assessment criteria matter not just in terms of understanding how threats are practically assessed in situations of school rampage threats, but provide insight into how school and police officials make sense of what is still an extremely misunderstood crime with an uncertain outcome.

In the very serious substantive incident at Adams High where Detective Brown was largely responsible for intervening during his time as an SRO, he could draw from the myriad evidence against the student plotter he arrested in order to gain the certainty that might otherwise elude him. He stated:

By the time we caught onto him, he says, "I didn't wanna do it anymore." We never will know if he was gonna do it or not. But he had the drawing [of him wearing the clothes he had picked out to wear on the day of the attack]. He had the hit list. And the map...There was also two suicide notes. Just more and more evidence. What else could this guy have shown us to say he was gonna do it?

In addition to this existent threat assessment criteria, the student in this case also broadly fit many stereotypical school rampage shooter profile characteristics (he was a male described as a being marginalized, suicidal, and fascinated with weapons, though he was half-Asian), and thus both elements of risk assessment converged in this case making it understandable for Detective Brown (and the two other respondents involved in this incident who were also interviewed) to feel a high level of certainty.

Certainty based on lack of threat assessment criteria

Just as the presence of myriad risk assessment criteria were valued in forging certainty about intent, certainty about a lack of intent was similarly high in the incidents where the evidence of detailed planning and preparation was scarce. This was true regardless of whether or not students had characteristics in common with school shooter profiles. In other words, if, as was the case in some instances (in which graffiti warnings were written on bathroom walls, students posted vague and unrealistic threats on social media websites, and lists of disliked people were interpreted as hit lists), proof amounted to a solitary piece of undetailed albeit threatening writing, very few officials believed that the threat at their school amounted to a serious and actionable plot. This was the case regardless of whether or not the accused students conformed to standard profiles. Such a finding is perhaps more surprising for cases in which students fit much of the stereotypical profile but which lacked the presence of threat assessment criteria (such as evidence of planning and weapons possession) than those cases in which students neither fit profiles nor indicated an abundance of threat assessment criteria. The analysis to follow will start with the less surprising latter variety where the lack of both forms of risk assessment criteria remained convergent and then move to the more interesting phenomenon present in the former variety of cases where the two types of assessment contradict one another.

As might be expected, school and police officials felt more certain about a lack of intent when there was a dearth of threat assessment criteria such as detailed planning and preparation. They especially doubted that students intended to carry out their plans when that lack of planning and preparation converged with students whose identifying characteristics did not conform to that of their expectations regarding what school rampage shooters are commonly believed to look or act like.

For example, in the incident at Jefferson Middle School, the principal, Mr. Anderson, shared his belief that even the presence of a hit list doesn't necessarily amount to a genuine risk for violence if the student deviates from stereotypical profile characteristics. As previously mentioned, gender played some role in how he determined that the preteen female student at his school was not a significant risk. In addition, Mr. Anderson noted that:

> This girl was not what I would call sick. She did not have a mental illness to the best of my knowledge. I'm not a psychologist, okay, but she was a typical teenage girl...and she made a big mistake. Big mistake. I mean I knew the parent. I had a good working relationship with the parent. This was not a kid that would have taken action on her words.

In addition to the fact that this case lacked much evidence of intent to carry out a rampage attack beyond the existence of the hit list, the principal noted that her mental stability, status as a typical teenage girl, and the principal's prior relationship with the parent all meant that she was not a genuine risk. Thus, he came to his conclusion about the girl's lack of genuine intent not only via threat assessment criteria (such as a lack of detailed planning and preparation), but through the consideration of conventional profiling characteristics regarding personal identity and her previous behavior history.

Notably, even when students fit numerous traditional profile characteristics, but lacked evidence of detailed planning and preparation, they were still given the benefit of the doubt and not viewed as genuine threats. For example, Mr. Cross was the principal of Hastings Jr/Sr High School where several students who could be understood as having traits in line with profiles (they were marginalized white male students who had been bullied) posted threats on a social networking website. He felt that:

> Our whole incident was totally blown out of proportion. I mean this group that we had, this so-called gang, they were calling themselves the Drive-By

Kings. They didn't drive! [*He laughs*] So that can tell you a little something about the whole thing.

He understood the students' threats to not be particularly genuine, at least in part, because of their lack of means to carry them out. Thus, the thought process of Mr. Cross is directly in line with that of O'Toole's (2000) threat assessment approach, wherein implausible unrealistic threats warrant the least concern and the substance of threats signify more than characteristics based profiles.

What's more, some administrators thought being required to proceed harshly (often as a result of zero tolerance policies) was inappropriate in the incidents at their schools due to the absence of extensive evidence of planning and preparation. In one case which took place at the affluent Greenvale High School, a student voluntarily left the school rather than facing expulsion after being accused and punished when a note cursing out many of his previous teachers was found and interpreted as a hit list. The Greenvale principal at the time, Mr. Sacco, stated:

> We had to go the full gamut. I was never convinced in my head he was ever a danger and never was. And it was one of the things where you had to act quickly and harshly with the risk you're going to alienate this kid more if you crush him too hard... The hit list was not a hit list in the true sense. It was his musings about fuck this and fuck that... He had lost of lists, lists of lots of things. He had a list of every teacher he ever had with the twist being the f-bomb planted in the middle of their name. So Mr. Sacco was Mr. Fucko... But, the so-called hit list really was something we had to act on as a school. I had to go through the whole thing, the expulsion, and, I'll be honest with you, I was never comfortable with that.

Mr. Sacco's reaction was not uncommon as numerous teachers and administrators whose schools experienced low-level threats with little evidence of planning and preparation (even when their students exhibited some profile characteristics) felt that parents and the media went overboard in characterizing them as dire risks or potential rampages. Additionally, cases such as this one indicate the value of, and likely support among some of the school community for, assessing threats in the manner suggested by Cornell (2013). That is, the punitive rubber stamp of zero tolerance needlessly treats all threats the same and thus punishes the majority of students excessively, and, in contrast, direct, detailed, and actionable plots ought to warrant more investigation and punishment than those of less severity.

Certainty based on threat assessment criteria in spite of deviation from profiles

A convergence of both forms of risk assessment criteria (profiles and threat assessment) led to a high degree of certainty among officials that students intended to carry out their attacks. Likewise, when cases failed to indicate evidence of threat assessment criteria, school and police officials generally did not consider threats to be serious whether or not the students fit profile characteristics. As a further testament to the broad acceptance of the threat assessment approach, there was still a high level of certainty present among officials when students who did not fit the profile of stereotypical school rampage shooters planned an attack which threat assessment criteria would deem a very serious substantive threat.

This exact phenomenon played out in the case at Everton High School, as the students accused were far from fitting the profile of stereotypical school rampage shooters. While they were white males, they were popular athletes very involved in school activities. At the same time, there was an abundance of threat assessment criteria to signify detailed planning and preparation. Initially, this contradiction between the two types of assessment criteria posed quite a dilemma for the school administrators and SRO attempting to evaluate the risk. Mr. Harris, one of Everton's house principals, revealed his confusion at the fact that:

> They weren't isolated. That was the scary thing. They did not fit what we thought was the profile for the kind of student that would plan something like this. They were engaged in school. They were involved in a sport. They seemed to have a large base of friends. They even had some popularity amongst the student body which was really bizarre.

When asked if the fact that the students did not necessarily fit the classic profile impacted his thinking in how to proceed and assess the seriousness of the threat, Mr. Harris responded, "Definitely. I mean we definitely noticed and were alarmed that they didn't fit the profile. It just didn't fit what we all believed to be the case about the kind of students that would do this sort of thing."

Another Everton house principal, Mr. Dougherty, confirmed that he also found it particularly difficult to take the threat seriously at first because of the type of students who were involved. He proclaimed:

> This is one of those things where people were saying that these guys were angry loners. They weren't. These guys were on the wrestling team. These

guys, when the wrestling team would be out running, they would be talking about Columbine…They looked like normal kids. I mean literally just looked like normal kids. They were on the wrestling team!…Looking at them, I will say this; when I heard it was the one kid who I had met before, I was like no way! What are you kidding? No way!…But as time passed and as things turned out, he was pretty into it.

Mr. Dougherty added that it took the evidence of planning present in the students' social networking websites that ultimately convinced him and the rest of the school community of the threat's seriousness. He said:

The news broke on Wednesday. During that next week, [the change in perception] was almost palpable in the building. The Thursday of that week, it was a joke. It's a joke, it's a joke, it's a joke. By Friday, the next day, it was kind of like you could sense the mood amongst the students and parents change. Because what ended up happening was obviously pretty much every kid and their grandmother went to the MySpace pages because they were still available…So as kids and parents looked at this stuff, by Friday, it was more like, wait, this wasn't a joke. It was palpable, this shift in the attitude of people here in the building.

Thus, the depth of planning evident from the websites convinced not only Mr. Dougherty and the other school officials to take the threat seriously, but the school as a whole. While they were initially more hesitant to see the threat as genuine because of the lack of stereotypical profiling characteristics, the weight of threat assessment criteria (i.e. the intricacy of the students' detailed plot) eventually changed their minds. Despite his initial skepticism, Mr. Dougherty eventually became the most emphatic of all respondents in his confidence regarding the students' intentions. He declared, "I am convinced to my dying day they were going to do something. There is no doubt in my mind."

Remaining uncertainty despite risk assessment

All of the aforementioned cases and quotations might give the impression that officials gained immense certainty and clarity by utilizing the threat assessment criteria, even if they could put less faith in the consistent validity of profiling stereotypical characteristics. This was not, however, entirely the case. Some school and police officials expressed significant doubt and uncertainty, even in cases with significant evidence of detailed planning and where students had obtained weapons.

For example, Mr. O'Brien, the vice principal at Courtside High School, initially stated that he and his fellow administrators deserved credit for "taking things seriously and investigating fully that led to us averting what could have been another Columbine, if not worse." However, he also gave considerable weight to the fact that the student plotter desperately wanted to get away from a father whom he deeply despised. After noting that his own personal experience meeting the student's father made it very clear how easy it would be to dislike the man, Mr. O'Brien noted that:

> [The accused student] stated to the police that he and his father did not get along. And that he was angry with him, and that's why he stole his gun. As far as we know, psychologically, we know that he had some issues... He didn't want to go home, that was the bottom line. He wanted to continue being placed somewhere, so it kind of goes back to that question about did he really plan on following through with this or was this his way of getting himself out of his house? Who knows what was happening there. So I don't know if he felt desperate enough to actually follow through and shoot some students, or if he was just going to see how far he could go until he got caught because he knew that would get him out of the school. I don't know. I don't really feel like I can say for certain. I know that this kid wanted help.

Thus, as the vice principal considered this alternative motivation for stealing the gun and calling negative attention to himself, he truly struggled with the student's genuine intent. Upon further reflection about the student in question, the vice principal then recalled an interaction that he had during trial proceedings in which the student appeared very apologetic. Mr. O'Brien discussed becoming increasingly uncertain that the student ever genuinely intended to go through with his plan in the first place. He noted that:

> When I was at the trial and the judge basically placed the student after I testified, and I walked by him, he said "I'm sorry for everything, Mr. O'Brien." So for him to say something like that tells me that, if I had to guess, I'd say he wasn't going to follow through, but he was certainly trying to get attention and he got it.

While Mr. O'Brien was not the only official to express doubts and uncertainty about students' ultimate intentions, he was the only one to thoughtfully address possible additional motivations for making a very serious substantive threat.

He was not, however, alone in his belief that expressions of regret might indicate a lack of genuine intent. In the case at Hastings Jr/Sr High, a guidance counselor at the school, Ms. Hanson, similarly emphasized the important role that she believed remorse played in her determination that the students never would have acted upon their threats. She pointed out that:

> I think the number one thing I look for is if they're remorseful or if they realize what they did was wrong. If they were in my office saying, "yeah, I did it and I'm going to still do it," that would throw up a red flag for me. But these kids were just shocked that they were getting called in for something they didn't really think was going to happen...It was just a couple of kids, wannabes, you know, trying to sound tough...I knew that it wasn't as serious as all the hype, just by talking to them that morning. I think that they knew that it kind of went overboard....I think they just thought they were being cool, making some threats here and there, but I don't think they realized it would turn into a three day shutdown with State Police helicopters landing here.

While expressions of remorse may potentially indicate a lack of intent, this cannot be considered a reliable criterion as numerous perpetrators of completed school rampages have voluntarily expressed regret and publically apologized to their victims and communities (see, for example, Goodrich 2012; Perez 2011; Verhovek 1999).

Conclusion

Ultimately, the threat assessment perspective gave officials the greatest confidence in their judgments deciphering if students intended to carry out their threats. This was demonstrated by the manner in which the greatest certainty abounded in cases where detailed planning and preparation were evident, regardless as to whether or not accused students fit traditional profile characteristics. That said, some officials still lacked full confidence in the infallibility of threat assessment criteria when they perceived alternative motivations for student actions and/or honest displays of regret on the part of students. These empirical findings are significant in revealing how risk assessment is currently understood and conducted in American public schools. However, it is hoped that the other issue to emerge from this research regarding officials' concerns with and hesitations about the certainty of risk assessment will also suggest the need to better comprehend and critically evaluate the purpose and goals of these practices as means of prediction, prevention, and/or punishment.

Risk assessments based upon individual and group characteristics remain controversial among scholars. This is due as much to the inaccuracies prevalent in early profiles and warning signs as to prior unrealistic expectations that any unifying and singular profile could emerge as a means of predicting future behavior. This study indicates that school and police officials generally share such skepticism about predictive profiles and warning signs, for while they may consider the relevance of said traits as a component of their assessments, such criteria was never deemed sufficiently convincing on its own. While few officials were aware of the empirical studies casting doubt on the reliability of school shooter profiles and warning signs, many were cognizant that these descriptions reflect statistical likelihoods rather than predictive certainties. Officials' additional confidence in threat assessment criteria may likewise reflect an aversion for the lofty and problematic objective of predicting school rampage threats and reveal potential opportunities to be found in the more achievable goals of preventing and punishing them. As recent threat assessment scholarship has explicitly addressed the distinctions between these goals, such promising developments warrant discussion.

The first emergent feature of the threat assessment approach is its newfound focus on prevention. All of the prior incarnations of risk assessment, including much of the early work on threat assessment, may be critiqued as a form "actuarial justice" (Feeley and Simon 1992; 1994) or what Young (1994) calls "administrative criminology" for being exclusively and perhaps inordinately concerned with the management and control of risky populations over and above the comprehension and alleviation of underlying forces which lead people to engage in violent and threatening behavior in the first place. In contrast, threat assessment scholars have called for a move away from prediction in favor of prevention in violence risk assessment. The former is seen as the ability to correctly estimate which people have the highest probability of being violent under which circumstances, while the latter shifts its emphasis to the most suitable intervention for the particular situation. Randazzo and her colleagues (2006: 153) made their case for this change in focus because "by emphasizing prevention as the outcome, the need to provide necessary services takes precedence over the need to be 'right' about whether a given child will become violent." Likewise, in his most recent scholarship, Cornell (2013; Cornell and Sheras 2006) has argued for a preventative approach to threat assessment, and even developed specific recommendations as to how to go about implementing such a preventative model for student intervention in schools.

Second, as threat assessment is constrained in its application only to those incidents in which individuals communicate threats in advance (Borum et al. 2010), its domain is limited to the consideration of comments and actions that have already occurred. Rather than positing that any group of identifying characteristics may be predictive (or even, on a less problematic scale, linked to a greater statistical likelihood) of future violence among populations who have yet to do any actual harm or break any laws by their broad resemblance to previous offenders, most threat assessment criteria are notable for also being criminal offenses themselves. As Daniels and his colleagues (2007: 92) revealed, students accused in these types of cases were often charged with crimes such as making terrorist threats, conspiracy to commit murder or aggravated assault, possession of firearms on school grounds, and interfering with an educational institution. Aside from these, additional charges (whose terms vary by state and thus are not all entirely distinct from those mentioned by Daniels et al. 2007) in my sample included criminal harassment, criminal intent to commit murder, threatening in the first degree, possession of homemade explosives, promotion of anarchy, and conspiracy to commit mass murder. Thus, threat assessment criteria such as communicating threats, forming detailed conspiracies, and weapons possession are all already criminalized, and the consideration of these factors amounts to a step away from the unrealistic aim of predicting the future via an extreme attempt at actuarial justice and toward the more realistic albeit conventional goal of punishing people for past behavior. As Officer Dudley said about one of the students he dealt with at Finley High:

> None of us will know if it ever would have went down, but it certainly had the potential to be a devastation...He deserves what he got because this wasn't just picking on somebody, this was conspiracy, and they terrified the whole school, the whole town.

Officer Dudley felt that while predicting students' ultimate intentions might be impossible, punishment was warranted in this case because of the actions they had already taken. This is not to say that the punishment/crime control paradigm is not without its own share of inherent flaws

(Clear 1994; Menninger 1968; Western 2007), but as the threat assessment approach emphasizes taking context and severity into consideration, its widespread adoption could lead to far more logical, proportionate, and equitable punishments and interventions than that of either statistical profiling or uniformly harsh zero tolerance policies.

4
Preventing School Rampage Violence through Student Bystander Intervention and Positive School Environments

Madfis, Eric. *The Risk of School Rampage: Assessing and Preventing Threats of School Violence.* New York: Palgrave Macmillan, 2014. DOI: 10.1057/9781137399281.0006.

The study of averted rampage has vital practical significance. By learning from the numerous instances where school rampage threats came to the attention of authorities and thus were thwarted, there exists potential for future policies and interventions to be modeled on prior successes. In addition, empirical knowledge about how school rampage incidents have been averted is especially important because many of the most popular and widespread school disciplinary policies and security practices implemented in recent years not only cannot be reliably linked to preventing rampage but also may actually hinder the few preventative measures with an empirical basis.

The findings to follow[1] reveal that it was people coming forward with knowledge about a prospective school rampage that has preempted these potentially deadly occurrences. However, even in many of these successfully averted incidents, numerous student bystanders, who were exposed to threats, still did not come forward; those who did were often not close associates or confidants of the accused students; and some who did ultimately come forward did so as a result of being personally threatened or in order to deflect blame away from themselves rather than out of altruistic concern for others. This suggests that schools have not seen as radical a progression away from the student taboo inhibiting information-sharing with authorities as previously asserted by scholars, practitioners, and the press. While numerous scholars and many of the school and police officials interviewed in this study acknowledge the important role that encouraging positive student bystander behavior plays in averting school rampage, few recognize how seriously ingrained the code of silence is among students. As a result, this chapter suggests that practitioners and scholars often overstate the degree to which students, after the extensive coverage that the Columbine massacre received, now take the threats of their peers seriously and report them to the authorities. Furthermore, the findings suggest that the lack of positive bystander behavior on the part of students likely reflects increasingly punitive and criminalized school environments that diminish trusting relationships between students and school staff.

School rampage violence prevention and the student code of silence

Since the infamous Columbine massacre, many short-sighted policies have been proposed and implemented in American public schools. The response has generally been the expansion of punitive disciplinary measures such as zero tolerance policies, enhancing surveillance via security cameras and SROs, and increasing security through target-hardening practices, such as limited entrances and metal detectors (Muschert and Madfis 2013). These solutions, however, lack empirical evidence confirming their preventative purpose and amount to short-sighted efforts to alleviate the anxieties of parents, faculty, and students. For example, schools continue to install security cameras and armed security guards specifically to prevent "another Columbine," yet both of these measures were already in place at Columbine High School and did not deter or prevent the killings there (Kupchik and Monahan 2006: 625). Schools across the country now typically lock all but one of their external doors during school hours as a safety precaution, though Adam Lanza easily shot through the glass windows at a locked entrance in order to gain entry into Newtown's Sandy Hook Elementary School (Flegenheimer 2013). Similarly, rampage killer Jeffrey Weise walked right through the metal detector at Red Lake Senior High School's front entrance. When a security officer confronted him, Weise promptly shot and killed the man (Meloy and O'Toole 2011). Zero tolerance policies were embraced widely across the United States by as early as 1993 (Skiba 2000). However, they did nothing to curb the increased number of multiple-victim shootings that occurred in middle and high schools across the nation in the late 1990s. As Cornell and Sheras (2006; Cornell 2013) have indicated, excluding students from school through expulsions and suspensions does nothing to resolve student problems or de-escalate conflicts, and such punishments have even exacerbated the existing isolation and anger of prior school shooters (Levin and Madfis 2009; Madfis and Levin 2013).

Empirical research on averted and completed school rampages, however, has begun to formulate an entirely distinct preventative approach. In her study of targeted school shootings, O'Toole (2000: 14) discussed the importance of a concept she named "leakage" that occurs when "a student intentionally or unintentionally reveals clues to feelings, thoughts, fantasies, attitudes, or intentions that may signal an impending violent act. These clues could take the form of subtle threats, boasts, innuendos, predictions, or ultimatums." Vossekuil et al. (2002: 25) discovered that at least one person had some previous knowledge about the plans of offenders in 81% of targeted school shooting incidents, while numerous individuals were aware in 59% of their sample. Of those people who possessed this crucial knowledge, 93% were peers of student perpetrators, such as siblings, schoolmates, or friends (ibid.: 25). Meanwhile, Gaughan and colleagues' (2001) national report discovered that only 54% of students said that they would inform an adult if they overheard one of their peers planning to shoot someone. These findings amplified discussions about a student "code of silence" which discourages students from coming forward with vital information about the dangerous intentions of their peers (Culley et al. 2006; Epstein 2002; Halbig 2000; MacDonald and Da Costa 1996; Merida 1999; Morris 2010; Stancato 2001; Spitalli 2003; Syvertsen et al. 2009).

The small number of studies that explore how prior incidents of school rampage have been averted (Daniels et al. 2007; 2010; Larkin 2009; Newman et al. 2004; Pollack et al. 2008) have generally located one common mechanism by which these potentially horrendous tragedies have been thwarted—students breaking through the code of silence to notify school and/or police officials about the violent intentions that prospective school shooters shared with their peers. Accordingly, schools have implemented anonymous e-mail systems and telephone hotlines to mitigate the problematic code of silence (Teicher 2006; Wilson-Simmons et al. 2006; Wylie et al. 2010) and employed various bystander prevention programs to encourage students to be more active about reporting problematic behaviors (Lodge and Frydenberg 2005; Twemlow et al. 2004). Moreover, Larkin (2009) has argued that, in the wake of Columbine, students have become more likely to report violent threats instead of acquiescing to the code of silence. In a *New York Times* interview about an averted rampage attack in 2001, criminologist James Alan Fox stated that "it shows that more and more students are willing to come forward and inform on classmates" and that, while snitching was unacceptable before the Columbine massacre, it is "now O.K., and is often the only thing to do when you can prevent a tragedy to classmates" (Butterfield 2001). Similarly, in their study of 15 student bystanders who had previous knowledge of four completed and four averted rampage attacks, Pollack and his colleagues (2008: 12) found that numerous students directly characterized the Columbine attack as a "wake-up call" after which threats were taken more seriously by youths increasingly willing to ignore the code of silence and inform authorities. Sharing this view, Delbert Elliott recently stated that, "It's a very good sign that the norm around 'snitching' or being a tattle-tale is changing" (McCrimmon 2009: 5).

In addition to the contention that peer pressure prohibiting "snitching" on other students has potentially decreased due, at least in part, to recent incidents of extreme school violence, Pollack et al. (2008) found that another facet of school culture was influential in determining whether or not students came forward when they were aware of information about threats. This study concluded that bystanders who alerted authorities "were influenced by positive relations with one or more adults, teachers, or staff, and/or a feeling within the school that the information would be taken seriously and addressed appropriately" (ibid.: 7). Additionally, students who exhibited a disinclination to come forward indicated that they anticipated negative responses from school officials if they were to share information. One student bystander did not come forward because he lacked a positive connection to anyone in a position of authority in the school and commented that he found them "too judgmental," while another student similarly indicated that he didn't tell anyone about the gun he knew was on school property because he anticipated being interrogated or getting into trouble for coming forward (ibid.: 12). This finding is congruent with plentiful research confirming the positive correlation between trusting, cohesive, and supportive school climates and student willingness to report threats of violence in both middle and high schools (Brank et al. 2007; Brinkley and Saarnio 2006; Fein et al. 2002; Syvertson et al. 2009: Wylie et al. 2010) and college and university settings (Sulkowski 2011).

That said, it has remained unclear to what extent the student code of silence has actually diminished in the post-Columbine era and what role positive bystander behavior and beneficial school climates have played in thwarting school rampage incidents since Columbine. Scholars also lack a clear understanding about the types of relationships that exist between the students who leak threats and those who come forward (such as close friends, acquaintances, or strangers), know little about the processes by which students come forward (anonymously or openly), and know almost nothing about which authority figures (such as teachers, administrators, counselors, and/or police officers) it is whom students confide in when they do reveal information. This chapter explores these questions through the detailed analysis of 11 instances of averted school rampage.

Unlike prior research that has relied upon content analysis of newspapers (Daniels et al. 2007; Larkin 2009) or interviews with student bystanders (Pollack et al. 2008) or school officials (Daniels et al. 2010), this study entailed triangulating data from legal documents, media accounts, and interviews with school and police officials. Accordingly, I am able to contrast how interested parties explain their perspectives on what led to successfully averted incidents with official documentation from the justice system and news media accounts. Such triangulation was essential as officials' perceptions of events did not always form a consensus with one another, nor with legal documentation or news reporting. While many details described by respondents about the cases can be tested against their colleagues as well as via legal documentation and media reporting, assertions about what occurrences and factors were most crucial in averting potential rampages are inherently subjective and open to interpretation. Thus, while, by and large, most respondents involved in the same incident agreed upon the basic elements of their case and how it was prevented generally, several emphasized distinct components as playing the most crucial role in the successful outcome. For example, each of the respondents involved in the averted incident at Finley High School credited his or her own connection to the case as being a vital factor, if not the crucial determining one. The police officer who arrested these students, Captain Dante, believed that they came forward at least in part as a result of the active shooter drill he conducted a few months before. He noted that "there was a lot of talk of the perpetrators of this crime saying, 'Jeez, the police are prepared for it now. Look what they did.'" Finley's principal, Mr. McGowan, believed the incident was prevented largely because of the trust built between students and staff at a leadership summit he organized, while both an SRO and adjustment counselor at the school discussed the role that their own rapport with the students played in making them more comfortable coming forward. This is not to say that any of these accounts are necessarily inaccurate, and they may in fact all reflect different elements of the same story. It is, however, important to recognize that all respondents experience events through their own lenses. Therefore, this study's multiple data sources enable a more detailed and nuanced understanding of the role of bystander involvement in preventing school rampage.

Perceiving a diminished student code of silence since Columbine

Numerous respondents discussed the student code of silence as vital factor in rampage violence prevention. Consistent with several scholars (Elliott in McCrimmon 2009; Fox in Butterfield 2001; Larkin 2009; Pollack et al. 2008), this was generally framed in the context of a new post-Columbine era wherein the code had been significantly diminished in response to extreme cases of school violence. For example, the head of school security at Adams High, Mr. Pullman, indicated that:

> I think one of the things that Columbine has done is it has broken in the old adage you know don't rat out your brother kind of a concept. And I think the kids are learning that there is some point when you should be saying something. Obviously, you're never going to get them to say everything, but I think the point has been made about the more important things.

Echoing this idea, Mr. Sacco, Greenvale High's principal, revealed how he believed things had changed since Columbine. He stated that:

> It absolutely made kids much more vigilant about things going on around them…I think it made kids less afraid to speak up if something wasn't sitting right with them. And since that era, I've often had a kid come by, and they're pained and they're tortured because they're thinking about that. They're thinking about could I have been carrying this around for an hour or two hours or three hours, and they'll say, "I've got to tell you this," and so I think that's the real good thing that's happened.

The principal of Blane High School, Mr. Cooper, felt that school lockdown drills, where students practice preparedness for a potential attacker, served to mitigate the code of silence as a reminder of the ever-present risk of school rampage. He asserted that:

> Lockdown drills serve as a reminder to students and staff, and students especially, that, unfortunately, in this day and age, we do need to be ready to try to go into a lockdown. If that helps students to be more aware, if they see something that doesn't sit right with them, then they might report that to somebody.

Thus, school and police officials repeatedly stated that, in the wake of Columbine, students were far more likely to come forward when they gained knowledge about their peers' intentions to do something harmful or dangerous.

Weakening the code of silence through positive school climate

In addition to declaring the significance of Columbine as a watershed event easing the stigma against students coming forward, there was near unanimity about the best methods to weaken the student code of silence; nearly all of the police and school officials articulated a strong belief in fostering supportive, cohesive, and trusting school climates—views very much in line with existing research (Brank et al. 2007; Brinkley and Saarnio 2006; Fein et al. 2002; Sulkowski 2011; Syvertson et al. 2009: Wylie et al. 2010). Nearly without exception, respondents emphasized the significance of creating an atmosphere where "students care about their school" because they "feel involved and part of the community," and "students feel supported" and "know they can trust the adults in the building" because of "predictable and consistent" "close relationships" of "dignity and mutual respect."

This pattern materialized in the abstract, as officials felt confident that a trusting school environment where kids feel safe confiding in the adults in their school building would ultimately mitigate future threats. For example, Kranston High's principal, Mr. Flaherty, said that:

> The best mechanism we have as a deterrent for these sorts of violent acts is good relationships between kids and adults, because kids will tell you. Kids will tell you when something happens. And if they saw a kid with a knife or they heard about it in the locker room...they'll tell you and that's the best security you can have, better than any policeman with a gun, better than metal detectors, better than locks and cameras. That's the best security...That is the best insurance you could ever buy.

On a more experiential level, this manner of thinking also emerged when officials explained why the specific incidents at their schools were averted. They frequently credited their schools' positive environment with making it easier for student bystanders to come forward with information.

In one instance that demonstrates this typical explanation, the vice principal of Courtside High School, Mr. O'Brien, stated that his current school exhibits a particularly trusting relationship, in contrast to another school he worked at previously, which had "a less respectful and collaborative environment, where what the principal said, goes." Courtside's principal, Mr. Fernandez, similarly emphasized the critical role of school culture when he described why their incident was prevented. He stated that:

> It was the result of a combination of relationships and taking things seriously and investigating fully that led to us averting what could have been another Columbine, if not worse...So the prevention factors were investigating fully and also having...a positive student culture where kids can talk to us and we can talk to them.

Blane High School's school psychologist, Dr. England, shared Mr. Fernandez's belief about the importance of positive relationships between students and school staff. When discussing the incident she dealt with at her school, she shared that:

> What happened was that students came forward and told us about [the threat], so I think the fact that there are connections, such close connections, between administrators and students here that you're much more likely to have students share that kind of information with you.

In addition to generally emphasizing the value of a positive school climate, some officials identified particular key aspects of their schools that helped diminish the code of silence. One Everton High house principal, Mr. Harris, emphasized the positive impact that lower student/faculty ratios and smaller class sizes played in building the sort of trusting environment which ultimately encouraged a student to alert school officials. Mr. Harris pointed out that, "We feel that smaller feel created better relationships for kids at their school and more of a connection and more care for their school. And that led to one student coming forward." Numerous other officials highlighted the rapport that specific individuals, such as certain teachers, SROs, and counselors, had with students. For example, when Courtside High's Principal Fernandez described the student who revealed information about his friend's plot to his teacher, he discussed the teacher in the following manner:

> The teacher was a favorite among the students. He's a young teacher...And students report that they like this teacher. They know that he works hard for them and that he cares about the school...I mean this is a guy who will volunteer for anything and go anywhere. He's a can-do kind of guy, and I've been able to depend on him for a number of different things. So he gets relationships with the students, and that's why he [the student who came forward] knew that he could trust him to do the right thing or genuinely help him when he shared the information.

Many of the authority figures initially entrusted with crucial information about potential attacks were similarly praised for demonstrating exemplary rapport. A counselor was said to possess a "supportive and caring personality." One SRO was described as follows:

> She was not someone you would think of as a police officer. She handed out lollipops. She was very, very easy to talk to. Not scary in the least bit, not strict and formal as you would assume a police officer to be. So she was

very caring and kind and very, very different than what you would assume a school resource officer to be.

Thus, according to the accounts of nearly all of the police and school officials interviewed in this study, the rampage attacks upon their schools were averted principally because of students coming forward due to trusting and supportive school climates where staff had created an inclusive sense of community. Closer scrutiny of the cases themselves, however, reveals a more complex situation and challenges claims about a greatly diminished student code of silence since Columbine.

Breaking the code of silence—interventions through leakage

Intervention as a result of leakage took four distinct forms in terms of the ways in which informants came to be aware of crucial information about threats and the types of relationships that existed between informants and the rampage plotters about whom they divulged informed. These categories included bystanders who indirectly gained information from students accused of school rampage schemes, trusted confidants who were informed directly of plans by accused students themselves, targets who were threatened directly by accused students, and co-conspirators who were directly involved, at least at some point and at some level, in the plots themselves. The discourse surrounding student leakage and the code of silence has heretofore only recognized the first two categories of intervention by student bystanders and confidants (though these have not been previously distinguished), and so the characteristics differentiating these groups warrant further clarification.

Indirectly informed bystanders

The most common form of intervention, which occurred in five instances (at Everton, Greenvale, Iverson, Jefferson, and Kranston), was through innocent bystanders who were not intentionally entrusted with secretive information by the accused students themselves, but who came to know the details about a rampage threat indirectly by inadvertently coming across hit lists, threatening web pages, or intimidating graffiti written on school property. For example, a student and casual acquaintance of the students accused of plotting a rampage attack against Everton High reported the disturbing posts and images on their social network website profiles to the SRO and an assistant principal. The Greenvale case came to light in a fairly analogous way, when numerous students informed school administrators that they observed one of their peers writing what they perceived to be a hit list of names in his notebook. Similarly, at Jefferson Middle School, a teacher notified the school principal after seeing one of her students writing a hit list on a piece of paper at the girl's desk. At Iverson High, a teacher and several students noticed a threatening message scribbled onto a wall in a boys' bathroom stall and informed the school principal. Likewise, Kranston High students noticed a threatening message written on a wall in one of their boys' bathroom stalls, and they informed teachers who in turn told the school principal and SRO.

Directly informed confidants

The second most common category of intervention occurred when those coming forward had gained direct information about threats as a result of being confided in by the students accused of plotting attacks. In the averted incident at Adams High, a student who had been sent threatening messages and video clips through the internet informing her of her friend's desire to attack his school led her to tell her mother who then called the local police department. When questioned by police, the accused student confessed his plans to commit a rampage attack and an arsenal of weaponry was discovered in his bedroom. In another case, several Blane High School students came forward to tell administrators that one of their peers had brought explosives to school with him. When school officials later searched this student's backpack, they discovered numerous explosives. Additionally, John, a Courtside High School student, stole guns from his father and gave them to his friend Tim to hold onto until they were needed to carry out the attack. John promised Tim that if he held onto the guns for him, he would not harm Tim or Tim's girlfriend. Tim did ultimately reveal John's plans to his parents. Tim's mother helped Tim get rid of John's weapons by throwing them into a local stream (an act for which she would later be prosecuted herself), and Tim's father later informed the school's principal and vice principal about John's plans to commit a rampage attack at the school. Shortly after being questioned by the school administrators and denying knowledge about the plot, Tim took it upon himself to tell one of his teachers about his complicity in John's plot. This teacher then immediately informed the school administration. In the case at Finley High, the girlfriend of one of the accused students alerted school officials about the numerous detailed threats made by one of her boyfriend's friends, though she did not come forward until after her boyfriend had already been accused of planning the attack by several of his co-conspirators.

Threatened targets

A third form of intervention occurred when people who had been threatened by students came forward to disclose this ominous behavior. Numerous scholars (Pollack et al. 2008; Reddy et al. 2001; Vossekuil et al. 2002) have found that targeted attackers who pose serious risks rarely threaten their victims in advance, but Meloy and his colleagues (2001) found that the majority of the adolescent mass murderers studied in their sample did, in fact, directly threaten their targets before committing crimes. The data in this study revealed two incidents (Donovan and Hastings) in which people who felt directly threatened by interactions with students accused of plotting school attacks alerted authorities to this threatening behavior, though only in the Hastings case did the threatening occur in advance and entail a student coming forward. The Donovan High School students tried and failed to carjack a vehicle, and police later arrested them while they were walking down a street with an arsenal of weapons. It was their potential carjacking victim, an adult stranger with no connection to the students or school, who alerted police. Perhaps as a result of the student code of silence, it is well established that juvenile victims in general are far less likely to report crimes committed against them to police than are adult victims (Watkins 2005). However, it was one of numerous students at Hastings Jr./Sr. High School who had been threatened by name on a social networking website by several other students who informed his parent of the troubling website exchange. This parent, in turn, called the president of the School Board to express concern.

Involved co-conspirators

Academic and public discourse has generally neglected to consider the role of co-conspirators who participate in developing a school rampage plot at some point and at some level, but who later come forward to prevent the attack from coming to fruition. The one exception is that of Larkin (2009), who noted that one of the participants in a rampage plot that was averted in New Bedford, Massachusetts in 2001 came forward because she feared for the safety of her favorite teacher. While incidents such as this, where co-conspirators come forward, may be more uncommon than any of the prior categories of intervention through leakage, the incident at Finley High School also followed this pattern. The sequence of events in this case is rather complicated, but as this particular incident seriously complicates and extends existing narratives about student bystander behavior and the code of silence, it warrants extensive elaboration.

The facts of this case begin when Tommy, a Finley student who would later be charged and convicted of conspiracy to commit murder and threatening to use deadly weapons, is discovered hiding a knife from his father during the course of an emotional outburst. Fearing that Tommy is suicidal, his father subsequently has him hospitalized at a psychiatric facility. Matthew, the other student later convicted on conspiracy charges, visits Tommy in the hospital. While there, Matthew becomes convinced that Tommy is being "brainwashed" and has abandoned their joint plan to attack the school along with two other students, Sean and Justin. Matthew makes an angry scene at the hospital in front of Tommy's family and girlfriend. After Tommy is released from the hospital, other students observe a positive change in his behavior. Eventually, Tommy and Matthew get into a fight with one another at a party, and Tommy tells Matthew never to speak to him again. According to Tommy, he also tells Matthew at this time that he hopes someone finds out about Mathew's plot.

Matthew then takes Sean and Justin, the other two student co-conspirators, with him to go speak to the adjustment counselor and later one of the SROs. Matthew tells both Sean and Justin not to speak during these meetings because he should do the talking, since he knows how to handle cops because his father is a police officer. Matthew then tells these school officials that they are all afraid of Tommy, who has been threatening them, mentioning how he wanted to acquire weapons and commit a rampage attack against the school. Both Sean and Justin go along with this plan out of fear of Matthew, who had assaulted Sean shortly before this at a party, and also because Matthew had threatened to cut out their tongues if they told anyone. Matthew subsequently blames everything on Tommy, while Sean and Justin concur in relative silence. During this time, Matthew assures Sean and Justin that they will get away with concealing their own involvement, and Matthew destroys evidence linking them to the plot. Police search Tommy's home and find maps of Finley High and lists of weaponry in his bedroom.

Much later, in front of the grand jury, Justin finally has a conversation with police away from Matthew and informs them of Matthew's actual deep involvement in the conspiracy. Sean and Justin are granted immunity in exchange for their testimony in the trial of Tommy. The prosecuting attorneys, arresting officers, SROs, and adjustment counselor all felt that Matthew went to the police because he believed he might get caught after his relationship with Tommy had deteriorated and he no longer trusted that Tommy would keep silent about their plan. In contrast, Matthew's defense attorneys argued that he abandoned his initial participation in the plot and actually stopped the attack from taking place (though they also denied that any of the accused students ever intended to carry out the attack in the first place). The defense's argument was ultimately unsuccessful in court and was not believed by any of the school or police officials interviewed in this study because of the fact that, when Matthew initially came forward, he had clearly lied to everyone in order to hide his true involvement in the plot.

The manner in which this case came to light in order to be averted does not fit in line with the typical rhetoric of an emergent willingness to break the code of silence as a result of Columbine or perhaps a positive school climate. Interestingly, several school officials who handled this case still credited their healthy school environment with how the incident was averted. Mr. McGowan, Finley High's principal, noted that:

> The bottom line is, it's about relationships. And when your kids feel comfortable being able to come and talk to you about stuff. We knew about it [the rampage plot] because of what happened in that Leadership Summit, and the fact that that kid trusted [the SRO] because she was with him for those two or three days, and he felt comfortable being able to come and say "I don't know if this is good."

One of the arresting officers in this case, Captain Dante, shared this sentiment. He stated that the school counselor and SROs:

> were close enough with the kids and built a relationship with the kids that they felt like they could sit down and tell them what was going on...when they thought twice, they went to somebody they felt comfortable talking to because they had built a relationship with them. And then I think that's the biggest thing.

However, it was not the case that students ultimately decided to turn to adults whom they trusted and reveal hidden plans to them. In fact, the plotters lied to the school officials when they came forward and denied their own involvement. This was not an example of a trusting environment encouraging innocent bystanders to come forward, but one in which three members of a school rampage conspiracy came forward to inform on the fourth member of their group in order to divert attention and the blame away from themselves.

How interventions occurred and who was trusted

All available information about these incidents indicates that when people came forward, they did so openly rather than anonymously. To some extent, this may reflect the fact that the incidents under investigation in this study ranged between 2000 and 2009 and anonymous reporting systems have only been implemented in the past few years—for example, one of the more prominent anonymous tip lines just began serving the state of Colorado in September of 2004 (McMillin 2009; Payne and Elliott 2011).

When people did come forward to reveal information to authorities, they were typically students (as in the cases at Adams, Blane, Courtside, Everton, Finley, Greenvale, Hastings, Iverson, and Kranston), though it was an adult who notified the police at Donovan High and teachers alerted school administration at Iverson and Jefferson. This supports Stueve and her colleagues' (2006) call for scholars to expand the definition of bystanders beyond students to include parents, teachers, and school staff members, because they may also possess information about potential violence. In this vein, parents also deserve credit for approaching the authorities in three cases (Adams, Courtside, and Hastings), as students in these cases revealed information to their parents before, or instead of, school or police officials.

More generally, beyond the three instances where parents were alerted, students informed SROs in two cases (Everton and Finley), administrators in four cases (Blane, Everton, Greenvale, and Iverson), counselors in one case (Finley), and teachers in two cases (Courtside and Kranston). It is only the instances in which students came forward to school or police officials that technically qualify as breaks in the code of silence. While these criteria apply in seven out of the eleven cases (Blane, Courtside, Everton, Finley, Greenvale, Iverson, and Kranston), the adult victim and teacher involved respectively in the cases at Donovan and Jefferson do not qualify, nor do the two instances (Adams and Hastings) in which students informed only their parents rather than school or police officials. This suggests that, in addition to the expanded notion of bystanders proposed by Stueve et al. (2006), perhaps scholars should similarly contemplate whether or not students who reveal information to their parents technically qualify as breaching the code of silence.

Following the code of silence—the persistence of bystander inaction

Even in the cases in which some students came forward—and that could subsequently be deemed successes in terms of illustrating positive examples of a broken code of silence—such an unequivocally rosy interpretation oversimplifies the truth. While student bystanders, trusted confidants, and targets deserve credit for individually coming forward and valuing school safety over student norms and concerns about status, positive bystander behavior on the part of a few students often occurred in the larger context of many more students keeping silent about their own knowledge of threats.

The occurrence at Adams High perhaps best illustrates this pattern, for while it is true that a female student is responsible for revealing the threatening behavior of one of her friends by informing her parents and then the police, many more friends and acquaintances of this accused student had been exposed by varying degrees to his disturbing comments and actions. In fact, the accused student in this case, Jessie, leaked various elements of his school rampage plot to a great number of his peers. When later questioned by the police, many of his fellow students acknowledged being aware of his deep fascination with the Columbine attack, as well as guns and explosives more generally. He had posted numerous references to Columbine on his social networking profile page, which many of his friends and school acquaintances had read.

Furthermore, several students indicated that he had showed them guns, maps, and/or bombs that he had constructed or detonated at some point prior. Jake, a close friend of the student plotter, said that, after fights with his parents, Jessie made comments about shooting up and using bombs in the high school. Jake added that when Jessie was angry, he would take out all of his knives and guns and lay them out from the smallest to the biggest on his bed. Jake also stated that he saw a map of the high school that Jessie had drawn in his bedroom. Jake said that Jessie discussed an attack once every couple of months, but indicated that he hadn't mentioned it for some time before he was arrested. Tim, another friend of Jessie's, reported that when Jessie got mad, he would sometimes say that he wanted to shoot the kids whose names he had listed on a sheet of paper, but Tim thought Jessie was only joking. Another student, Anthony, said that throughout the previous fall and spring, Jessie sometime talked about how cool it would be if something like Columbine would happen at their high school, and he said that, if it happened there, he hoped that black and gay people would die. Jessie indicated to Anthony that he would shoot these people if he could, and then he told him that he wanted to shoot up the high school, Columbine style, at the end of their sophomore year. Anthony thought Jessie was joking when he said these things because he would always laugh during or after he said them. Yet another student, Jennifer, said that in the previous spring, Jessie joked that he wanted to bring a gun to school and kill all the kids he hated at lunchtime. She indicated that he brought up this idea of a school shooting many times but always said he was joking. Roughly a month before he got arrested, Jessie said to Jennifer, "Don't go to school tomorrow." When she asked him why, he repeated, "Don't go to school tomorrow. I like you." Jennifer stated that after this exchange, Jessie said that he was only joking, though she later admitted that she understood this to mean that he was talking about committing a Columbine shooting in the future.

As Detective Brown, the SRO directly involved in this incident, commented, "These are all different people, interviewed separately, that are saying the same thing...which makes you wonder why no one said anything." Thus, at least four students entrusted with intimate knowledge about Jesse's intentions as his confidants did not come forward to reveal what they knew until after Jessie had been arrested. When only one in five students (and these four were merely those that the police had extensive knowledge about because they were willing to provide testimony) came forward to the authorities, this is perhaps more of an indication of the continued resilience and power of the student code of silence, rather than a success story of a school somehow breaking through the code via a positive school atmosphere.

Adams High was not alone in illustrating this problematic trend, as many other instances which could potentially be praised for illustrating positive bystander behavior or broken codes of silence actually revealed, upon closer inspection, many more examples of leakage that had gone unnoticed, dismissed, or ignored. One Everton High student came forward to the school's SRO and then to a house principal to inform them of his friend's nefarious plans. However, several other students had been asked to join in on the murderous plot; they declined not only to participate in it, but also to inform any adults about its existence.

The four student plotters at Finley High attempted to recruit at least two other students to participate in their conspiracy to attack the school. While these students rejected the offer to join the group of student plotters, none of the reticent would-be recruits ever came forward to reveal what they knew to school or police authorities. One of the SROs involved in this case, Officer Dudley, stated that:

> We had at least fifteen witnesses that did statements in this case...This evolved from nothing and all of a sudden you've got fifteen kids that knew about this for the last year and a half. And it turned out that a couple of the kids that were key to the verdicts failed to be recruited...and some of those kids turned out to be our best witnesses...But nobody came forward until these boys came forth [to blame their conspiracy on one of their accomplices].

In addition to the students they tried and failed to recruit, one member of the conspiracy also told a female student that if anything were to happen, she would be safe because he considered her a friend, and several other female students were explicitly informed about their plans to shoot up the school without expressly being invited as participants. As previously mentioned, only one of these female students came forward to school officials, and this only took place after initial accusations had already been made.

The Courtside High student plotter intended to tell several of his friends not to go to school on the date he planned to carry out his attack, though it is uncertain how many others knew but did not come forward. Likewise, in the cases at Blane, Greenvale, Hastings, Iverson, and Kranston, some students came forward, but it is uncertain from all available information how many other students knew about these threats or plans in advance who did not do so. At Donovan High and Jefferson Middle School, it was adults rather than students who came forward to alert authorities, and it is also unclear if any student bystanders, confidants, or targets were aware of, or subjected to, their peers' threats.

Implications of findings

Ultimately, the findings above confirm previous research and reporting about the manner in which it is people coming forward with important information gained via leakage that leads to rampage attacks being averted. They also reveal that the dominant approach to school violence deterrence via punitive disciplinary policies and enhanced security did not play a prominent preventative role. These events were not deterred due to the presence of metal detectors, locked doors, security cameras, or SROs. In fact, many of the student plotters considered these developments to be minor stumbling blocks easily resolved through additional preparations among already detailed plans. For example, some plots entailed killing or disarming officers and bringing weapons into the school buildings before entrance doors would be locked for the day. Additionally, though the logic of zero tolerance is similarly deterrence based, wherein strict punishments for threatening behavior or possession of weapons in school would dissuade students from these activities, most of the schools where rampages were averted displayed some elements of zero tolerance (though support for the approach varied widely), and all of them were subject to the mandate of the 1994 Gun Free Schools Act wherein bringing a firearm to school warrants a mandatory year-long expulsion. Thus, these myriad and copious deterrence-based strategies cannot be credited with thwarting these homicidal threats. However, the data do indicate that SROs can play a preventative if not deterrent role in averting rampage, as it was SROs whom students trusted enough to approach in two cases (Everton and Finley, though the latter incident is less indicative of a genuine display of trust), and they did help garner vital confessions from accused students at Adams, Courtside, and Everton.

In addition, the findings suggest that numerous potentially lethal rampage attacks were prevented, at least in part, as a result of school cultures being sufficiently positive for students to feel comfortable telling school authorities about threatening behaviors that concerned them. However, school officials at Finley High credited a positive school culture for averting the attack, even though this was undoubtedly not how the incident played out. The same could be said for Adams High, where the head of school security praised his own school's positive school culture, when it was actually a student from another town and school district who actually came forward to the authorities, while none of the students at his school who were exposed to leakage did so. Thus, there may be some tendency on the part of officials to attribute undue credit for averting these incidents to positive school climates.

Certainly, students breaking through the code of silence still constituted the major manner by which most events have been thwarted. That said, close inspection of the details of these cases indicates a murkier and less-optimistic picture than the one painted by scholars (Elliott in McCrimmon 2009; Fox in Butterfield 2001; Larkin 2009; Pollack et al. 2008) and generally recognized by the school and police officials interviewed in this study, many of whom agreed that the student code of silence drastically diminished in the wake of numerous highly publicized rampage shooting attacks such as the one at Columbine High School. It seems that both scholars and practitioners came to this conclusion through media reporting (such as Bower 2001; Butterfield 2001; Robertson 2001) upon numerous recent incidents where rampage plots were averted as a result of students coming forward with information gained through leakage. However, by carefully investigating incidents of averted rampage in detail, two distinct elements of the findings of this study suggest previous conclusions based upon superficial accounts in the media are at best premature.

First, those who came forward were not uniformly close friends and confidants of student plotters; they were also mere acquaintances, the victims of threats, and even the conspirators themselves. MacDonald and Da Costa (1996) found that students were more willing to report victimization if the perpetrator was not a friend of theirs, and Pollack and his colleagues (2008: 13) noted that one of their student respondents came forward in part because of the fact that "he was not close friends with the potential attackers so that allowed him to be more objective when he learned of a possible attack plan." Thus, it should perhaps not be entirely surprising that authorities are often alerted to the presence of rampage threats by people less close to the accused perpetrators. This does suggest, however, that a student code of silence among close friends remains a significant challenge. Second, this concern about students maintaining secrecy in their most personal friendships is exacerbated by the fact that many of the adolescents exposed to leakage who were the closest to the students accused of plotting attacks did not in fact come forward to authorities. More generally, in several cases the number of students exposed to the leakage of their peers who did not ultimately come forward exceeded the number of students who did come forward.

Thus, while some scholars and media coverage have depicted even one student who comes forward and has any type of relationship to an accused plotter as evidence that the code of silence has diminished, this narrative is complicated when one considers the actual relationships between student bystanders and plotters as well as the rarely reported on but numerous students who have not come forward even in these averted incidents.

Therefore, if scholars want to interpret these averted incidents as an indication that the student code of silence has diminished, it is worth considering more specific measures or levels of both leakage and code-breaking (i.e. positive bystander intervention by students). Meloy and O'Toole (2011: 525) suggested that researchers need more sophisticated studies of leakage that explore the various forms it takes in order to ultimately discern which, if any, are the most "predictive of actual targeted violence." In the same way, breaks in the code of silence are not uniform and should not be depicted as such by scholars proclaiming their significance and increased occurrence. It may be the case that students who come to be directly informed of threatening information by their closest friends are exposed to the most profoundly significant form of leakage. It is almost certainly the case, however, that these close confidants who then share that knowledge with authorities engage in a far more substantial breech in the code of silence than students who come forward after being targeted themselves or who only know the students they are accusing as distant acquaintances. Thus, instances in line with the former type (such as at Adams, Blane, and Courtside) constitute a far better indicator of a broken student code of silence than instances of the latter types (such as at Everton, Greenvale, Hastings, Iverson, and Kranston),[2] though all of these latter cases do demonstrate some indication of a willingness to break through the code. At the same time, when only one student comes forward though many more possess information about a threat of violence (as was documented in the Adams and Everton cases), this should not be counted as equivalent evidence of a broken code of silence as would an incident in which multiple or even all students with relevant information came forward. Thus, future scholarship on both leakage and the code of silence must consider these nuanced distinctions in order to properly measure and understand the role that both phenomena play in averting school rampage and other forms of targeted school violence.

Conclusion

The findings of this chapter suggest that, while students' coming forward with important information about threats constitutes the key manner by which rampage attacks are thwarted, a student code of silence persists beyond the previous expectations of academics, police officers, and school officials. This aligns with Wylie and colleagues' (2010: 351) contention that "[a]lthough policies aimed at improving school climate may increase a student's willingness to report and are important in their own right, improving a school's climate may be a daunting task." Syvertson and her colleagues (2009: 230) point out that decades of bystander research suggests potentially "scores of reasons," aside from strict adherence to a code of silence, which help explain why students do not intervene when confronted with dangerous situations. Bystander scholarship highlights the importance of diffused responsibility, the disinclination to intercede while part of a group because individuals anticipate that others will respond instead (Mathes and Kahn 1975). As numerous students were aware of the threats made in several of these cases, it is feasible that some students neglected to come forward because they expected their peers to do so. The bystander literature also stresses the role of ambiguity about the situation (Latané and Darley 1969). Students may not approach adults if they lack certainty about their peers' intentions and interpret legitimate threats as flippant comments or jokes. Though student inaction related to leakage likely results from a combination of these forces (Pollack et al. 2008), and much work remains to be done in the realm of student bystander awareness and education generally, the findings of this chapter reveal an important misunderstanding in how many practitioners and academics discuss healthy and successful school environments.

Copious empirical evidence (such as Brank et al. 2007; Brinkley and Saarnio 2006; Eliot et al. 2010; Fein et al. 2002; Sulkowski 2011; Syvertson et al. 2009; Wylie et al. 2010) indicates the relationship between supportive, trusting, and cohesive school climates and positive student bystander behavior. Thus, the problem is not so much that educators and scholars mistake the significance of a beneficial school climate. The problem is that they are largely mischaracterizing the atmosphere of contemporary American public schools. Despite institutional objectives of inclusiveness and the beneficial role of certain especially kind and empathetic school and police officials, any candid examination of recent developments in American schooling reveals a substantial trend away from empathy, inclusivity, and supportiveness, and toward the enhanced security and punitive discipline that Hirschfield and Celinska (2011) call "school criminalization" (see also Hirschfield 2008; Kupchik 2010; Kupchik and Monahan 2006; Lyons and Drew 2006; Monahan and Torres 2010; Muschert and Peguero 2010; Nolan 2011). The increased use of law enforcement personnel, mindsets, and technologies in schools, as well as the increasing transfer of school discipline to the juvenile and criminal justice systems (Advancement Project 2005; Kim, Losen, and Hewitt 2010; Wald and Losen 2003), have direct consequences upon the overall school climate. As Casella (2001: 35) fittingly described, such "policies...bolster punishment in favor of pedagogy, control in favor of understanding." The result is that many of these features diminish trusting relationships between students and school staff (Lintott 2004; Noguera 1995; Watts and Erevelles 2004).

This lack of trust has direct consequences for the prevention of school rampage. Syvertson and her colleagues (2009: 229) describe the dilemma eloquently when they conclude that:

> In this post-Columbine era, public education has seen an increase in zero tolerance policies...It is possible that these policies create an environment that actually discourages students from revealing their concerns to teachers because of the increased "costs" of revelation...For most adolescents, divulging a peer's confidence is a difficult decision that may be intensified by a zero tolerance climate. As was reflected in our findings, the more students believed that going to a teacher or principal would result in trouble, the more likely they were to ignore a peer's dangerous plan or to simply tell a friend (but not an adult).

Similarly, Cornell (2013: 393) recently explained that, "Students may be more willing to report threats when they see that school authorities are not taking a punitive, zero tolerance approach, but are instead concerned with solving problems and preventing conflicts from escalating into violence."

School criminalization diminishes positive bystander behavior not only as a result of lost trust due to excessive punitiveness, but the perception that such discipline is prejudicial may similarly result in fewer students coming forward. Morris (2010: 270) proposed that "if students perceive strict or invasive school discipline as biased, they might resist school authority more vehemently, increasing the social distance between students and the school." It has been widely documented that African

American youth are vastly overrepresented in school suspensions and expulsions (Casella 2001; 2003; Civil Rights Data Collection 2012), even when socioeconomic indicators are held constant (Skiba et al. 2002), and when their punishments are compared directly to white students who committed identical infractions (Fenning and Rose 2007). Even zero tolerance policies, formed at least in part with the goal of objectivity in mind, have resulted in disproportionate application toward minority students (Kupchik 2010; Robbins 2005). To the extent that students perceive school discipline as fundamentally unjust due to racial prejudice, they will be far less likely to entrust school and police officials with vital but potentially incriminating information.

Consequently, even though many of the recent measures focusing upon punitive discipline and enhanced security were designed specifically to improve school safety in the event of a rampage attack (Muschert and Madfis 2013), these very practices significantly hinder the one means by which nearly all rampage attacks are actually thwarted—positive bystander behavior on the part of students aware of leakage. Kohn (2004: 26) deftly clarifies the most significant point here when he states that such punitive policy "isn't merely ineffective—it's actively counterproductive." Therefore, doing nothing in response to fear of school rampage would have been preferable to many of the authoritarian practices schools have put in place.

In order to prevent future attacks from occurring, schools must abandon these punitive measures and improve upon the means by which these events are actually averted, by forging genuinely positive school climates that encourage student bystanders to intervene in a responsible manner. In this regard, there are numerous emergent approaches to discipline and punishment which may actually improve school climates in exactly the manner necessary to increase trusting relationships between students and school staff, thus potentially resulting in far more positive bystander behavior and, accordingly, far less successful incidents of school rampage. Numerous schools across the United States and internationally serve as positive examples of how to utilize the rapidly expanding knowledge from restorative justice in their everyday applications of school discipline through practices of group conferencing, peacemaking and sentencing circles, and victim/offender mediation. In these practices, the conventional goals of deterrence and punitive retribution are replaced by a focus upon the restorative goals of reconciliation, reparation, and transformation (Van Ness and Strong 2010). In perhaps the most extensive text on the subject of restorative classroom discipline, Meyer and Evans (2012) describe its key characteristics as inclusive and encouraging learning communities that utilize positive behavior management to resolve conflicts, solve problems, and restore harms with clear definitions of appropriate behavior and a consistent application of consequences.

Sherman and Strang (2007) found that, when directly comparing people who received restorative justice interventions to those who did not, victims faired considerably better on a variety of outcomes and offenders demonstrated lower recidivism rates, especially for violent crimes. In addition to these positive outcomes more generally, schools that have implemented restorative practices have seen increases in attendance, declines in suspensions and expulsions, and even dramatic decreases in bullying and school violence (Karp and Breslin 2001; Meyer and Evans 2012; Sumner et al. 2010). These positive outcomes notwithstanding, the crucial element pertaining to the findings of this chapter is the numerous studies which have consistently found that restorative school practices have the ability to strengthen positive school relationships by fostering inclusive school climates, improving student perceptions about the fairness of punishments (i.e. procedural justice), and increasing student trust in school authority figures (McCluskey et al. 2008; Mirsky 2003; Morrison 2007; Sherman and Strang 2007; Sumner et al. 2010; Youth Justice Board 2004). These are precisely the sort of outcomes needed in order to minimize the likelihood that marginalized students will feel the sort of extreme exclusion often necessary to build up the desire to commit a rampage attack against their school (Levin and Madfis 2009). However, even if this improved school climate fails to prevent students from engaging in the planning of homicidal plots, the student peers in these school communities will be far more likely to report any and all information revealed to them through leakage. In fact, one of the schools investigated for this study, Courtside High School, has recently received a great deal of praise and attention as a leading exemplar of restorative school practices and has experienced substantial improvements in the school's climate and reductions in disciplinary problems, including violence. It is perhaps notable then that Courtside was highlighted above as an example of the most noteworthy and substantial variety of breaking through the code of silence (i.e. directly informed confidants) when a student divulged his close friend's plot to school authorities.

Thus, as it is crucial to adopt school policies and procedures that encourage positive bystander behavior on the part of students, it is vital for schools to adopt restorative and ameliorative practices in place of the punitive forms of discipline and security that remain currently dominant in American educational institutions. This is essential as the prevailing approach not only fails to prevent and deter school rampage, but the school climates of exclusion, retribution, fear, and mistrust that such policies breed actively discourage positive bystander behavior and permit the student code of silence to persist.

Notes

1. Some sections of this chapter have been substantially revised from an article previously published in the journal *Youth Violence and Juvenile Justice*.
2. The Donovan and Jefferson cases involved adults coming forward rather than students so neither represents a breach in the student code of silence. While the particulars of the Finley case may also disqualify it from counting as an example of breaking the code, the averted New Bedford case indicates that co-conspirators coming forward may still constitute code-breaking under some circumstances.

5 Summary of Findings, Policy Implications, and Future Research

Madfis, Eric. *The Risk of School Rampage: Assessing and Preventing Threats of School Violence.* New York: Palgrave Macmillan, 2014.
DOI: 10.1057/9781137399281.0007.

Through in-depth interviews with school and police officials (administrators, counselors, security and police officers, and teachers) as well as content analysis of news reporting and legal documentation covering 11 averted incidents of school rampage in the Northeastern United States, this study has explored perceptions of and reactions to threats of multiple-victim school attacks. Given the dearth of empirical scholarship on averted incidents of school rampage, this research unearths important data on the process by which threats of rampage violence are assessed and how previous school rampage plots have been averted.

This study furnishes valuable insight into the institutional cultures and policies conducive to the effective obstruction of rampage attacks. Subsequently, this research reveals the significant shortcomings and sometimes harmful consequences of contemporary risk assessment, violence prevention, and punishment practices prominent in American schools. By examining averted incidents, this work addresses problematic gaps in school violence scholarship and advances existing knowledge about mass murder, violence prevention, bystander intervention, risk assessment, and disciplinary policy in school contexts.

Summary and implications of findings

The initial data chapter, Chapter 2, contributes to the literature on violence risk assessment in two distinct ways. First, the in-depth analysis of 11 incidents reveals great diversity among even this limited sample, and thus indicates the dire need for future scholars to adopt clearer distinctions and stricter operationalizations when using terms such as "threat," "risk," "plot," and especially when characterizing any event as "averted." Secondly, the findings showcase the wide-ranging manner by which school and police officials make discretionary decisions about how to assess the severity of student threats. Assessment criteria entail how detailed a plot was (including who was to be purposely targeted, what locations were to be attacked in what order, and when the attacks were to take place), the role of weaponry (such as the existent, potential, or desired access to weapons, evidence of weapons training or manufacture, and threats specifically mentioning the use of weapons), individual traits (including ethnic/racial and gender identity as well as previous behavior and mental health concerns), and group characteristics (specifically school social status and affiliations with deviant subcultures). The fact that some of these criteria are substantially more supported with empirical evidence than others reveals a clear need for increased education and programming to better inform school and police officials about the best practices of violence risk assessment.

Chapter 3 explores which forms of risk assessment provide school and police officials with the most confidence in their determinations. Though numerous respondents did believe in, and utilize, some problematic and stereotypical profiling characteristics to help them make decisions, they ultimately placed their greatest confidence in threat assessment criteria, such as evidence of detailed planning and preparation to commit an attack. Many previous studies have revealed the empirical successes that the threat assessment approach has demonstrated in the appraisal of targeted violence threats over other forms of risk assessment (Borum et al. 2010; Cornell 2013; Reddy et al. 2001). This finding suggests, in addition, that threat assessment may also be credited for an intuitive appeal which leaves officials more confident that justice has been properly served than is the case when the same officials rely upon comparatively more nebulous forms of statistical prediction through identifying profiles.

In the fourth chapter, close scrutiny of the 11 averted incidents indicates that both scholars and educational practitioners overestimate the extent to which the student code of silence has actually been diminished post-Columbine. This does nothing, however, to lessen the perhaps more significant emergent finding that it is most frequently students coming forward with knowledge about their peers' violent intentions that has led to rampage attacks being averted. This has considerable implications for the future administration of school safety in that, while some schools have adopted bystander intervention programs and enacted anonymous tip lines, these solutions have largely taken a back seat to more punitive disciplinary policies and enhanced security measures. As zero tolerance policies, metal detectors, surveillance cameras, and other law enforcement solutions cannot be credited with either deterring or preventing the crimes in these cases from being planned let alone committed, their utility and prevalence warrants serious reconsideration. Additionally, as restorative approaches to school discipline have been shown not only to reduce violence but to improve school climate in a way which encourages students to come forward to authorities when they have been entrusted with crucial information about an impending attack, such alternatives warrant far more consideration if not widespread adoption.

DOI: 10.1057/9781137399281.0007

The data, taken as a whole, result in numerous significant implications. First, when officials in districts with relatively low rates of crime and violence overestimate the occurrence and likelihood of school rampage and base broad policy decisions on these devastating events, their risk calculation is not only statistically inaccurate but also rhetorically dishonest. The public, including school and police officials as well as students and parents, ought to be engaging in a debate over whether or not the negative aspects of punitive zero tolerance policies and enhanced security (such as changes to the school atmosphere as an educational institution, potential violations of students' civil liberties, and expenditures of limited resources for security personnel and technology) are worth the benefits of reducing or preventing typical and relatively minor student misbehavior, rather than having to conduct a cost-benefit analysis where one side of the equation is characterized in such a radically skewed manner (i.e. the cost of not adopting law enforcement and other punitive solutions in schools will immanently result in multiple students deaths).

Secondly, the findings of Chapter 4 amplify such concerns over a school safety discourse disconnected from rampage prevention policies that have an empirical basis. Not only did the aforementioned punitive measures not play a decisive preventative role in the 11 incidents under investigation in this study, but multiple prior studies suggest that these measures negatively impact the most common means by which school rampages are actually prevented by making students less trustful of adult authority figures and thus less likely to come forward when they possess knowledge about potentially dangerous situations.

At the same time, the findings of this study also necessitate careful consideration of the potentially negative consequences to occur if the student code of silence were to entirely dissolve. While a broken, or at least diminished, student code of silence may mean that numerous future plots will be brought to the attention of authorities and pre-empted, it also may carry with it a problematic effect on the overall school environment. It is vital that genuine substantial threats are taken seriously, but a suspicious and fearful school culture that overestimates the likelihood and normalcy of rampage violence threats, and encourages students and teachers to come forward with even minor concerns about students' dangerous thoughts, questionable actions, and overall violence potential, amounts to a rather unwelcoming learning environment.

The academic conversation on school criminalization, while notable for its critique of expanding forms of directly oppressive surveillance and punishment, neglects, by and large, to consider the ways in which evolving school violence prevention practices also encourage informal and indirect types of coercive control, in particular, the governing of conduct via student surveillance of themselves and their peers. With regard to this development, Foucault's scholarship proves extremely enlightening. Foucault (1977) famously argued that societies would ultimately move away from formal institutions of social control and toward less official but more omnipresent informal varieties of surveillance and coercion. The main thrust of this proposition has yet to prove accurate, as recent decades have seen rapidly expanded levels of incarceration in general (Alexander 2010; Pattillo et al. 2004) and, in the school setting, the advent of a "school-to-prison pipeline" in which school misbehavior is punished through the juvenile and criminal justice systems rather than in the educational system (Advancement Project 2005; Kim, Losen, and Hewitt 2010; Wald and Losen 2003). Despite this, Foucault's later work (1980; 1991) has been utilized in recent discussions of the sociology of risk to explain how individuals come to take the task of surveillance upon themselves in order to regulate and manage their own behavior and that of others (Mythen 2008). In particular, his argument regarding the ubiquity of more subtle and coercive forms of control and surveillance is extremely relevant in understanding the potential drawbacks should the student code of silence dissipate in the context of exaggerated risk perception regarding school rampage.

For example, a controversy at a Kansas high school revealed the potential problems of a risk discourse which over-anticipates rampage violence and consequently encourages students to inform school and police authorities of any potential knowledge about a hypothetical threat. When a student with a grudge against five of his classmates falsely claimed that they planned to shoot up their school, this student's bogus story was widely believed by school authorities, though not by the majority of the student body, and all five supposed plotters were arrested (Logan 2002). More recently, in the wake of a school shooting in Chardon, Ohio on February 27, 2012, rumors widely circulated among high school students from another Ohio town that accused one bullied teenager of planning to bring a gun to school on the following day, which would have marked one week after the Chardon shooting. Though this led police to search the boy's home and caused half of the student body to be absent on the day in question, it was ultimately determined that he was entirely innocent (Leitsinger 2012). Emergent developments such as anonymous tip lines may more easily side-step concerns with the student code of silence, but they may also lead to many more instances of false accusations.

Encouraging students to break through the code of silence and school and police officials to take students seriously when they do come forward is certainly a more productive and empirically driven approach than reactionary measures such as zero tolerance policies, security cameras, and metal detectors. However, even this reaction may present some troubling manifestations where peers are less trusting of one another, false accusations become prevalent, and relatively benign comments on the part of students may be misinterpreted and subjected to overzealous scrutiny. That said, if we collectively reject the pessimistic view of actuarial justice that school rampage violence is an inevitable phenomenon, then perhaps we can broadly implement restorative approaches toward negotiating conflicts and dealing with student misbehavior in order to create inclusive and supportive schools and even begin to envision a larger society which adopts broad-based ameliorative solutions to the original social strains leading to these conflicts and misbehaviors in the first place.

Suggested areas for future research

Through the exploration of the averted school rampage phenomenon undertaken in this study, numerous avenues for future research have come to light. As the topic remains in its infancy with regard to empirical scholarship and even careful conceptual scrutiny, important questions remain.

It is vital that the scholarship on averted school rampage be expanded with larger samples in order to gain a more representative picture of the problem and how schools have reacted to it. Distributing surveys to a large random sample of school and police officials would go a long way toward indicating the extent to which the findings in this study are generalizable to the population at large. For example, surveys exploring what violence risk assessment practices are currently utilized by school and police officials and eliciting opinions regarding the perceived efficacy of those assessments would be enlightening and important. Because of the significance of the threat assessment approach indicated in this study, there would perhaps be the greatest utility in nationally representative studies of the threat assessment approach that measure not only its perceived efficacy but also its outcomes when utilized in a preventative manner. In addition, my findings indicated that the forms of risk assessment utilized by school and police officials varied to some extent by their job types. This qualitative conclusion, however, can only be considered preliminary, and so a larger quantitative survey exploring these variations in a representative manner would prove useful. There is much the same need for nationally representative surveys of school disciplinary policies and security measures, both in terms of how prevalent various forms are, and how officials perceive their effectiveness.

Additionally, as the present study was limited to averted rampages in the Northeastern United States, future scholars should expand to other regions of the country. This is especially important as both averted and completed school rampages are actually more prevalent elsewhere, with the most incidents occurring in the Southern and Midwestern states (Trump n.d.; Kimmel and Mahler 2003). It also remains unknown whether or not school rampages are perceived, assessed, and responded to differently by geographical regions with distinct political and cultural traditions. For example, my respondents were nearly unanimous in their condemnation of calls to arm faculty members in schools via the scaling back of concealed carry firearm restrictions, but this may reflect a Northeastern predilection for gun control that would be far less dominant in other parts of the country.

Beyond the American context, school rampage incidents have also been averted in at least two widely publicized incidents in Manchester, England (Carter 2009) and Cologne, Germany ("Attack on German" 2007). However, international cases of averted rampage have never been systematically studied, even in the superficial manner necessary to provide a basic indication of their prevalence. In addition to an international comparative study of averted rampage incidents, scholars ought to fully investigate international variations among responses to school rampages. In the aftermath of many school attacks in the United States, Americans have witnessed calls to arm students, teachers, and faculty members, either as a means of deterring future offenders from making an attempt or with the mindset that an armed populace would be able to more easily stop a rampaging killer. In fact, nearly 20 American states considered new legislation to permit students and faculty to carry firearms on college campuses in the wake of a recent massacre that occurred in Tucson, Arizona on January 8, 2011 in which 19 people, one of them U.S. Representative Gabrielle Giffords, were shot (Gottesdiener 2011). While the 2012 massacre at Sandy Hook Elementary School in Newtown, Connecticut did spark debates about background checks and limiting magazine capacities, American policy discussions in recent years have rarely focused upon reducing the access to, or availability of, firearms. By contrast, the most common reaction to rampage incidents outside of the United States (e.g. in Germany and Australia) has been attempts by gun control advocates to reduce teenagers' access to deadly weapons. Thus, international comparative research has the potential to reveal great insight into the manner in which anti-violence policy is often the result of particular cultural, political, and structural manifestations rather than the uncontested or inevitable solution to particular crises.

While no scholarship has explored averted incidents of school rampage outside of the United States, recent research on completed school rampage incidents beyond the American context (Madfis and Levin 2013) discovered that none of these international school rampage incidents involved students killing in pairs or in groups (like the killer duos of Westside Middle School in Arkansas and Columbine High School in Colorado), while more than one student was accused in five out of the 11 averted incidents in this study (Courtside, Donovan, Everton, Finley, and Hastings). This suggests that it may be the case that the more student plotters involved in a particular incident, the more leakage there will be, and thus the more likely it will be that the students will be caught. However, further in-depth case study research with a larger sample would need to be conducted in order to confirm the existence of this possible relationship.

Finally, averted school rampage can be situated as one subset of the larger phenomenon of averted acts of violence and crime, and thus these findings would be fruitfully compared to similar studies of other prevented transgressions. Averted incidents of mass murder outside of the school setting warrant investigation (as only White-Hamon 2000 has addressed this topic). Likewise, it would be worthwhile to explore whether or not other forms of attempted mass murder (such as workplace avengers, family annihilators, and disgruntled citizens) were thwarted via similar means as those school rampages investigated in this study. It is unclear how frequently adult mass murders display leakage and inform others about their dangerous intentions. Though adults who have been informed about the homicidal plans of a would-be mass killer may not be subject to a student code of silence, they may still be distrustful of law enforcement and/or perceive of "snitching" as an unacceptable violation of the "code of the street" dominant in low-income and minority communities (Anderson 1999; Morris 2010; Rosenfeld et al. 2003). Thus, comparing the role that intervention by the confidants of adult rampage killers played in averting multiple homicides to that of school rampages averted by peer confidants coming forward would prove insightful. Likewise, though adults are not systematically assessed and monitored in the way that schools do to their students, adults with developed and actionable plans to harm many people en masse may similarly engage in leakage or otherwise raise concerns among their family members, friends, coworkers, mental health providers, or other acquaintances. This suggests that there may well be value in exploring the role of leakage in incidents of mass murder outside of the school setting.

More broadly, researchers have neglected the much wider phenomenon of attempted and averted incidents of single-victim homicide, even though it's a far more commonly perpetrated and prosecuted crime than averted rampage. The same may be said for advancing the conceptual and empirical understanding of all attempted crimes, for while this has long been an interesting area of debate in law and philosophy (see, for example, Adams 1998; Arenson 2005; Bayles 1982; Becker 1973/1974; Christopher 2004; Davis 1986; Duff 1997; Enker 1977; Feinberg 1995; Ohana 2007; Spjut 1987; Yaffe 2010), the topic has been broadly overlooked by sociologists and criminologists. Even those explicitly exploring the popular topic of crime prevention (such as Clarke 1995; Rosenbaum et al. 1998; Sherman et al. 2002; Trembley and Craig 1995) have neglected to consider how criminal attempts might inform preventative measures. While the existing foci upon understanding the root causes, risk factors, and situational determinants of crime all surely help prevent future offenses, there may be a wealth of knowledge as yet unearthed about the deterrence and hindrance of crime to be gleaned from the study of averted incidents.

6
Methodological Appendix

Madfis, Eric. *The Risk of School Rampage: Assessing and Preventing Threats of School Violence.* New York: Palgrave Macmillan, 2014.
DOI: 10.1057/9781137399281.0008.

This study utilized multiple strategies in the research design. The first stage of research entailed searching the *LexisNexis* newspaper database as well as the internet and various academic and governmental publications in order to gather the population of publically reported school rampage plots that occurred in American public schools from 2000 to 2009 which were discovered before the perpetrators had the opportunity to commit them. These quantitative data provided a background understanding of the extent of the phenomenon and its variation by region. After collecting the population of these events, the next stage of research involved contacting principals at schools around the Northeast to request interviews with them and various other school and police officials (administrators, counselors, security and police officers, and teachers) who were directly involved in preventing the potential violence. This stage was necessary in order to glean data regarding perceptions of, and reactions to, violent threats, violence prevention, and school security. Employing this research strategy was necessary for the exploratory investigation of a fairly new and understudied phenomenon, and it resulted in a wealth of descriptive data triangulated with news reports, court transcripts, and arrest records to assure accuracy.

Operationalizing school rampage and averted threat

Before going in-depth about the mechanics of data collection, the purpose and process of operationalization in this study must be addressed as the definition of a "school shooting," and even the more specific term "school rampage," have varied substantially across numerous publications. First, it is vital to note that the notion of an averted rampage leaves room for a wide range of severity between various cases wherein students' genuine desire to complete a rampage attack is perhaps problematically assumed. For example, scrawling a vague threat referencing Columbine on a school bathroom wall and stockpiling an arsenal of weaponry are both actions that could be classified as evidence of an averted rampage, though the actual level of threat present in these two scenarios varies a great deal (Reddy et al. 2001). Cornell et al. (2004) distinguished between "transient" threats made carelessly in jest or in a moment of anger and the more serious "substantive" threats where genuine harm is intended, and found that only 30% of their sample of school violence threats were of the latter more concerning type and a mere three incidents were deemed genuine threats worthy of expulsion. However, as a main goal of this research is to explore how threat is perceived and assessed by school staff, all cases of potentially violent threats of school rampage were included regardless of the magnitude of evidence present.

Since the highly publicized multiple-homicide attacks of the late 1990s, school shootings have often been thought of as events with multiple victims, though most murders on school grounds are actually single-victim homicides (Hagan et al. 2002). Thus, some recent scholarship has moved away from the all-encompassing "school shooting" term to specifically discuss "rampage" events with multiple victims (Muschert 2007; Newman et al. 2004). In the literature on homicide, the traditional definition of a "mass murder" limits the phenomenon to those events wherein at least three victims were killed during a single episode at one or more closely related locations (Duwe 2007; Fox and Levin 2011; Holmes and Holmes 2001). While viewing multiple-victim school attacks as a subset of the larger mass murder phenomenon has certain conceptual benefits (Levin and Madfis 2009), such a focused definition permits little analysis of cases which have not resulted in multiple deaths (Madfis 2014b). Individuals with the desire and intent to kill numerous people yet who fail to do so only because their plans come to the attention of authorities before they are to be carried out or those who severely injure many people but fail to do so fatally have been excluded from prior operationalizations (White-Hamon 2000). These less-successful perpetrators may be distinguishable by their overall incompetence with weaponry and/or their inability to maintain secrecy about their future actions, but not necessarily by their original motivations and goals.

Thus, there is a certain conceptual utility in including all cases which involve an attempt to kill numerous people in the study of mass murder (White-Hamon 2000). Such cases of attempted school mass murders were included in the sample for this study, though "successful" cases where perpetrators fatally injured multiple victims and those where perpetrators injured multiple victims but failed to kill them were excluded. Numerous prior studies have addressed the nature and extent of completed mass murders in general (Duwe 2004; 2007; Fox and Levin 1994; 1998; 2011; Holmes and Holmes 2001; Levin and Fox 1999; Meloy et al. 2001; Meloy et al. 2004; Palermo and Ross 1999; Petee et al. 1997) and at schools in particular (such as Harding et al. 2002; Levin and Madfis 2009; Moore et al. 2003; Newman et al. 2004; Newman and Fox 2009; Vossekuil et al. 2002) and it is hoped that future studies will focus upon

failed but not averted school mass murders where numerous victims have been non-fatally injured (see Sullivan and Guerette 2003 for one case study), but these events fall out of the scope of the current research.
Additionally, Newman et al. (2004) limited her definition of school rampage to those school shootings in which multiple people were killed or injured on school property by a student or recent former student of the targeted school and only those cases in which at least some of the victims were chosen in a random and indiscriminate manner. This definition has numerous assets, but also various problems. As mentioned previously, limiting the scope to multiple victims proves helpful in crystallizing the phenomenon and distinguishing it from other types of school shootings. This study similarly limited the cases under investigation to the actions of those committed by current or former students, rather than utilizing Muschert's (2007) larger net for rampage shootings which also includes the homicidal misdeeds of current and former school employees.

The Newman et al. (2004) definition of rampage becomes somewhat problematic when the subject one desires to study is students' foiled plots to commit multiple-homicide at their current or former schools, as these authors limit the phenomenon to school "shootings" where firearms were the predominant weaponry. Numerous deadly plots formed by students over the past ten years have involved bombs, explosives, and even knife attacks (Trump n.d.). Though not all were detonated, bombs were a vital component of the Columbine High School killer duo's plan (Larkin 2007), and the most deadly mass murder at a school in American history involved dynamite and hundreds of pounds of pyrotol, but no firearms (Bernstein 2009). Accordingly, all manner of plots to commit multiple murders on school grounds were included, regardless of the perpetrator's intended weaponry.

Newman and her colleagues' (2004) latter qualifying criterion of random or symbolic victims also proves rather nebulous. This distinction has similarly caused Muschert (2007) to distinguish between "targeted" and "rampage" school shootings—the latter of which necessitate random or symbolic victims. While the typological distinction has a great deal of value as it is important to distinguish between symbolic attacks on institutions and targeted attacks on individuals, limiting data collection to include only rampages with random or symbolic victims seems premature for this study of averted mass casualty events at schools. Previous mass murders at schools (and elsewhere, for that matter) have variously included victims who were individually targeted, victims specifically selected due to their group membership or social status, victims chosen randomly for their symbolic significance as representatives of an institution, and random victims harmed merely to increase the overall body count (Larkin 2007; Vossekuil et al. 2002). Perpetrators have killed across these categories during a single episode (Fox and Levin 2011). As the empirical literature is currently too underdeveloped to definitively conclude that distinct victimological categories inevitably correspond to distinct school shooter typologies or motives, cases which seem to lack symbolic or random victims were not operationally eliminated from investigation. This was especially salient during the initial stage of investigation via newspaper and internet accounts where offender-victim relationships were rarely discernable. Thus, cases which qualify as averted school "rampages" (Daniels et al. 2007; 2010; Newman et al. 2004; Muschert 2007) planned by former or current students with multiple specific and nonspecific victims will be included in the operational definition used in this study as well as those which would be deemed attempted "targeted school shootings" (Muschert 2007) with multiple specifically intended victims.

Prior academic definitions have variously limited school rampages by the type of weaponry, by the offender's connection to the school as former students, current students, staff members, or strangers, by the relationship between offenders and victims as specific or random targets, and by the number of victims killed or injured (Daniels 2007; 2010; Levin and Madfis 2009; Moore et al. 2003; Muschert 2007; Newman et al. 2004; Newman and Fox 2009; Vossekuil et al. 2002). In order to preserve as general a concept of rampage as possible while still maintaining a focus upon the assessment of student threats, this study has defined averted school rampage plots as those cases of any form of fatal violence planned by one or more students targeting multiple specific or nonspecific classmates and/or faculty at their former or current school which was pre-empted from occurring and causing any death or injury and of which there is any evidence of intent.

Research design and sample

I first located cases through the *LexisNexis* newspaper database. Similar to Daniels et al. (2007), the search terms included "school" and "plot*,"[1] "school" and "rampage*," and "school" and "shooting*," though the additional terms "school" and "attack*," and "school" and "threat*" were added. Cases which occurred outside of the United States were excluded as were any incidents which involved adult strangers and former or current school staff as perpetrators, those which focused upon colleges or universities as desired targets, and those events which resulted in any injury or death or where only one victim was intended. In addition to the cases located through the newspaper database, numerous academic and government-sponsored publications (such as Larkin 2009; Newman et al. 2004; Virginia Tech Review Panel 2007), popular press sources (Bower 2001; Lieberman 2008; Robertson 2001) and various internet sites which compile lists of school violence incidents (Brady Center n.d., "List of School-Related Attacks" n.d.; Trump n.d.) were consulted to gather a comprehensive list and to confirm the accuracy of data across multiple sources. By this method, 195 cases of averted school rampage attacks which occurred in the United States from 2000 to 2009 were located. These quantitative population data for the entire nation were collected for descriptive purposes to look at the quantity of school rampage threats, and how they vary by geographical region. This information advances knowledge in this area substantially because, while Kimmel and Mahler (2003) found that school rampage attacks occur, by and large, in politically conservative suburban and rural communities, no previous data exist regarding the geographic distribution of averted rampages.

The next stage of data collection was exploratory qualitative research which involved contacting the middle and high schools that experienced and averted rampage threats in the past ten years. To make the project a manageable size and to facilitate as many face-to-face, in-person interviews as possible, the sample was limited to schools in the Northeastern United States (a geographical area which includes the New England states, New York, New Jersey, Pennsylvania, and Delaware). Of the 195 cases nationwide, 29 incidents occurred in Northeastern schools. To facilitate access, I mailed a letter to the 29 current head principals at these schools, informing them about the intended study and requesting permission to conduct interviews. I then emailed and/or telephoned the principals in order to once again request access and to set up a date to conduct interviews with them and any other staff members who possessed personal knowledge of the averted incident.

At the start of each individual interview, I provided further details about the purpose of the study and the respondents' informed consent. Respondents were notified that they could stop the interview at any time, could skip any question for any reason, and should avoid disclosing any information about criminal activities unknown to the authorities. In addition to my verbal explanation, all of this information was included in a written consent form provided to respondents who were interviewed in person, while respondents interviewed over the telephone were emailed copies of the consent form, if they desired them. Though the interview method could not permit anonymity, I did promise confidentiality to my respondents by assuring them that no publications to arise from this research would contain the names of any individuals or schools who participated, and every effort will be made to conceal identifying information.

Of the 29 head principals contacted, 11 were willing to permit me to conduct research about the incident at their school. Three principals refused participation in the study, and the remaining 15 principals never responded to my repeated attempts to contact them via telephone and email. This may be partially explained by job turnover in that my data went back to the year 2000, and many current principals and staff members were not working at the schools in question when the incidents occurred (an extreme example of this was that one of the principals in charge during the course of an averted incident was later removed for having an illicit relationship with a student). For some of the cases that had taken place most recently, school administrators were not permitted to speak with me about incidents where hearings and trials were still ongoing. Other rationales for non-participation might be explained by concerns about school reputation, external scrutiny, or simple time limitations (one high school principal informed me that he only agreed to participate because he was impressed by the dedication I showed in calling and emailing him repeatedly over a period of numerous weeks). In the only available information on averted school rampage that exists to serve as a basis for comparison, Daniels et al. (2010) found that only four out of the 13 schools they contacted would consent to participation. Pollack et al. (2008) did not reveal their specific response rate for student bystanders or schools involved in averted incidents, but only 15 out of the 29 students they discovered who were involved in either averted or completed rampages agreed to be interviewed.

Though two of the 29 schools originally contacted were private institutions, all of the 11 schools that granted me permission for interviews were public institutions. As the demographic information to follow (which comes from the 2000 census as well as local community and school websites) indicates, these 11 schools were all located in predominantly white regions of the country, and though one incident occurred at a lower middle class school in a rural area, the rest of the schools under investigation were located in suburban areas with largely middle class and affluent populations.

Adams High School is located in a middle class suburban community where 93% of town residents are white, household median income is roughly $57,000, and 3.5% of the population is below the poverty line. Of the nearly 1,500 students at the high school, 16% receive free or reduced-price lunch.

Blane High School serves students in an affluent suburban community where 93% of the population is white, median household income is upwards of $80,000, and 2.1% of the population is below the poverty line. Of the more than 1,500 students at the high school, 5% receive free or reduced-price lunch.

Courtside High School is located in a community with a population that is 72% white, household median income is just under $36,000, and 11.3% of the population is below the poverty line. The school serves roughly 800 students, 45% of which receive either free or reduced-price lunch.

Donovan High School is located in a suburban borough where 86% of residents are white, median income for households is just above $43,000, and 6.1% of the population is impoverished. Of the approximately 800 students at the school, 26% are eligible for the free or reduced-price lunch program.

Everton High School is a large suburban school of nearly 3,500 students, 4% of whom are eligible for free or reduced-price lunch. In the town as a whole, 92% of residents are white, 3.7% are below the poverty line, and median income for a household is roughly $75,000.

Finley High School, a suburban school with roughly 1,300 students, has 6% of its students receive free or reduced-price lunch. The town is 93% white with 0.9% of the population below the poverty line, and a median household income of roughly $84,000.

Greenvale High School is located in one of the most affluent suburban communities in the nation. In the town where this school is located, 95%

of the population is white, the annual median income for a household is more than $140,000, and about 2.5% of the population is below the poverty line. Approximately 1,300 students attend the school, but no data on how many of them receive free or reduced-price lunch is available.

Hastings Jr./Sr. High School is a combined middle and high school in a rural town. The school has an enrollment of roughly 600 students, 41% of whom are eligible for free or reduced-price lunch. The borough where the school is located is 99% white, median income for a household is just below $27,000, and 15.6% of the population is below the poverty line.

Iverson High School is an affluent suburban school that enrolls more than 1,200 students, 4% of whom are eligible for free or reduced-price lunch. The town in which the school is located has a population that is 92% white, 3.9% under the poverty line, and household median income is more than $145,000 per year.

Jefferson Middle School serves nearly 800 students, 20% of whom are eligible for free or reduced-price lunch. It is located in a borough that is 87% white, has a median household income of nearly $61,000, and where 3.6% of the population is below the poverty line.

Kranston High School is a large school in a suburban town. The school has an enrollment of more than 2,000 students, and 23% of them are eligible for free or reduced-price lunch. In the town, 73% of residents are white, median income for a household is more than $54,000, and 16% of the population is impoverished.

Many of the principals who agreed to be interviewed also referred me to other individuals at the local schools or police departments who could provide additional insight into the offenders, their threats, and the reactions of the schools and communities. In all, I spoke to 32 people (17 administrators, four counselors, seven security and police officers, and four teachers) associated with these 11 incidents at schools across the Northeast. Seventeen of these were conducted in person at respondents' schools or police departments, and the other 15 interviews took place over the telephone when this was the respondent's preference or when on-site interviews could not be coordinated. To triangulate the data gleaned from these interviews and to confirm the accuracy of what my respondents told me, I cross-checked their accounts of an incident against their colleagues' accounts of the same incident, as well as with newspaper reporting, and whenever possible, court transcripts, legal briefs, and police incident reports.

Complications of relying on the news media to build a sampling frame

Certain limitations exist by relying on news media accounts to gain a sampling frame of averted school rampage plots. In Duwe's (2000) study of how the print news media report mass murder, he found that the most widely publicized mass murders nationwide were disproportionately likely to include large numbers of casualties, victims unknown to the offender, public locations, assault weapons, interracial offender-victim relationships, older offenders, and workplace violence. Cramer's (1995) study found a similarly biased focus upon gun use in news media accounts of mass murder. Hence, a list compiled from newspaper searches may result in a disproportionate number of cases that fit these descriptions. No similar studies have investigated this bias in the school context and my data are already intentionally limited to plots of multiple-casualty events in public locations. However, if such a finding may be generalized to school rampage plots, this may mean that my data would similarly suffer from an inordinate number of cases where students have targeted victims of different races or ethnicities, as well as from undue attention paid to rampage attacks with random victims rather than targeted attacks and an overrepresentation of school shooting plots, as opposed to schemes involving bombings, knives, or other weaponry.

In addition, Duwe (2007: 185) found that only 45% of mass murder incidents were reported in the *New York Times*. Likewise, Cornell et al. (2004) indicated the presence of 188 violent threats during one school year in 35 schools across a single county in central Virginia, so there is no question that numerous threats go unnoticed and unreported by the media. Though only three of these 188 incidents were deemed genuine threats (wherein students were expelled for planning violence against particular students), they did locate another 16 cases "involving multiple or nonspecific victims" (Cornell et al. 2004: 537). Nearly three dozen cases in one county during the course of a single year far outnumbers anything found via previously published articles or newspaper accounts, but this high number can likely be explained by the fact that these 16 events were not deemed sufficiently serious to necessitate law enforcement intervention and thus gain media attention.

Finally, there is anecdotal evidence (McGabe and Martin 2005: 88) that showcases how school administrators responded "quickly and quietly, as the school system did not want parents or the media notified [to] an emotionally disturbed student [who] had compiled a 'hit list' of students" to shoot and kill. As it is often in the interest of principals and other administrators to maintain good reputations for their schools, it should not necessarily be surprising that they would wish to hide potentially embarrassing stories from the media. Accordingly, there are potentially numerous cases of rampage threats which have been handled internally by school officials and thus never publicized by the media.

On qualitative methodology

The research strategy employed in this study enabled not only the descriptive investigation of the extent and placement of rampage attacks, but a diverse and in-depth exploratory inquiry into how school rampages are manifested, perceived, and prevented. This is a necessary first step, as little prior scholarship has focused upon the form and content of averted rampage plots. Qualitative methods are uniquely well suited to the study of new phenomena about which little or no previous research has been conducted, as they allow for the identification of new concepts and concerns via inductive discovery, rather than by forcing respondents to express themselves only within the confines of preexisting terminology with preset questions and hypotheses. Furthermore, while the content analysis of newspaper stories is an informative source with which to explore background data on the substance of these incidents, the interpretation of threat and risk are ultimately subjective endeavors which necessitate qualitative methods better suited to "make sense of or interpret, phenomena in terms of the meanings people bring to them" (Denzin and Lincoln 2005: 3). As such, the best method to conduct research which carefully investigates the complex motivations, risk calculations, symbolic meanings, and thought processes by which school officials determine their attitudes and beliefs about violent threat assessment and prevention is in-depth interviews with the school officials tasked with such responsibilities. The thoughts and perspectives of a small number of people examined closely will prove more fruitful in the understanding of common underlying processes and the formulation of theory than a comparatively superficial, albeit more generalizable, look at a larger sample of the population (Athens 1992). Additionally, triangulating information on averted rampage threats by cross-checking multiple sources is surely the best way to assure the integrity and accuracy of data.

Violent school threats and the manifold ways in which they are perceived, assessed, and prevented are naturally complex and subjective topics which previous theoretical formulations of crime, violence, and fear in other contexts cannot fully explain. Utilizing an inductive approach, this research did not test specific hypotheses upfront, but rather resulted from the formation of conceptual schemes which were explored and investigated so that patterns naturally emerged (Schutt 2004). After the data collection stage, I used a grounded theory approach (Charmaz 2001; Glaser and Strauss 1967) in order to inductively derive typological categories and themes through the process of coding interview transcripts with the ATLAS.ti software program.

Generalizability in qualitative research

A common critique of qualitative methods is that the conclusions drawn from small non-random samples cannot be generalized to the population at large. With regard to this study in particular, my sample is not strictly representative of, nor are its results generalizable to, all averted rampages in the classic quantitative sense. Though I started with as close to the population of averted rampage incidents as possible, those willing to grant me access to their schools may have been running better environments less complicit in the creation of school cultures where students want to engage in rampage attacks in the first place. Additionally, the fact that my interviews were limited to the Northeast means that we still know little about similar incidents in the rest of the country or the world at large. This is particularly significant because the majority of both attempted and completed school shootings have taken place in the Southern and Midwestern regions of the United States.

However, acknowledging the inability of qualitative work to achieve classical notions of generalizability because of a lack of large random samples, some scholars have attempted to form alternative conceptions more useful for qualitative research (see Schofield 2002 for a detailed review of some recent developments in meta-ethnography, the case survey method, and the qualitative comparative method). One of the more famous may be found in the work of Guba and Lincoln (Guba 1981; Guba and Lincoln 1982; Lincoln and Guba 1985), who favor the term "transferability" to replace the goal of context-free laws desired via generalizability. In their conceptualization, analytic leaps across times, people, and places are desirable but permissible only under particular circumstances which may be assessed if sufficient thick description is available "to make a reasoned judgment about the degree of transferability possible" (Guba and Lincoln 1982: 247). Still other qualitative researchers view generalizability as "unimportant, unachievable, or both" (Schofield 2002: 173) and reject it as a goal because every subject "must be seen as carrying its own logic, sense of order, structure, and meaning" (Denzin 1983: 134). Whether or not this same critique applies to the newer qualitative notion of transferability, qualitative studies still maintain their underlying significance, as whatever they lack in generalizable knowledge of those outside the site of interest, they more than make up for with analytic generalizability (Kleinman et al. 1997) as a force to formulate knowledge on "larger generic theoretical concerns" (Sanders 2004: xi). Particular behavioral motives, patterns, and outcomes are best understood in complete context, but theoretical constructs transcend their specific circumstances. For example, the conflict between Cohen's (2002) infamous youth subcultures, the Mods and the Rockers, and a public which was so fearful of and fascinated by them, must be situated in post-war English class relations and the demography of youth at the time, but his theoretical construct of moral panics need not be. Thus, while qualitative research may be less useful for specifying definitive beliefs or behaviors that apply across peoples and locales, it is vital for the generation of new insights, particularly in areas of research which have been understudied. While the manner in which threat is constructed, manifested, and perceived will surely vary across school districts, between regions of the country, and over time, the analytic categories, discourses, and relationships unearthed by this study's detailed qualitative investigation of violent school threats may prove useful regardless of the time or setting.

Note

1 These asterisks (*) allow for increased search results as they enable results to include any words starting with what comes before the asterisk. For example, a search for "plot*" will not only come up with results for the words plot, but plotter, plotting, plotted, etc.

References

Adams, David M. 1998. "The Problem of the Incomplete Attempt." *Social Theory and Practice* 24: 317–343.

Advancement Project. 2005. "Education on Lockdown: The Schoolhouse to Jailhouse Track." Retrieved June 5, 2012 (http://www.advancementproject.org/sites/default/files/publications/FINALEOLrep.pdf).

Aitken, Stuart C. 2001. "Schoolyard Shootings: Racism, Sexism and Moral Panics over Teen Violence." *Antipode* 33(4): 594–600.

Alexander, Michelle. 2010. *The New Jim Crow: Mass Incarceration in the Age of Colorblindness*. New York: New Press.

Altheide, David L. 2009. "The Columbine Shootings and the Discourse of Fear." *American Behavioral Scientist* 52(10): 1354–1370.

American Bar Association. 2001. "Zero Tolerance Policy Report." Retrieved September 20, 2010 (www.abanet.org/crimjust/juvjus/zerotolreport.html).

American Psychological Association. 1999. "Warning Signs: A Violence Prevention Guide for Youth." Retrieved September 30, 2010 (http://helping.apa.org/warningsigns/index.html).

American Psychological Association Zero Tolerance Task Force. 2008. "Are Zero Tolerance Policies Effective in the Schools?: An Evidentiary Review and Recommendations." *American Psychologist* 63(9): 852–862.

Anderson, Elijah. 1999. *Code of the Street: Decency, Violence and the Moral Life of the Inner City*. New York: Norton.

References

Andrade, Joel T. (Editor). 2009. *Handbook of Violence Risk Assessment and Treatment: New Approaches for Mental Health Professionals.* New York, NY: Springer.

Andrade, Joel T., Katherine O'Neill, and Robert B. Diener. 2009. "Violence Risk Assessment and Risk Management: A Historical Overview and Clinical Application." Pp. 3–40 in *Handbook of Violence Risk Assessment and Treatment: New Approaches for Mental Health Professionals*, edited by Joel T. Andrade. New York, NY: Springer.

Arenson, Kenneth J. 2005. "The Pitfalls in the Law of Attempt: A New Perspective." *The Journal of Criminal Law* 69(2): 146–167.

Arluke, Arnold, and Eric Madfis. 2014. "Animal Abuse as a Warning Sign of School Massacres: A Critique and Refinement." *Homicide Studies* 18(1): 7–22.

Aronson, Elliot. 2004. "How the Columbine High School Tragedy Could Have Been Prevented." *Journal of Individual Psychology* 60: 355–360.

Athens, Lonnie H. 1992. *The Creation of Dangerous Violent Criminals.* Chicago: University of Illinois Press.

"Attack on German High School Prevented, Police Say." November 18, 2007. Retrieved May 8, 2012 (http://articles.cnn.com/2007-11-18/world/germany.school.plot_1_school-shooting-web-page-german-police?_s=PM:WORLD).

Ayers, William, Rick Ayers, and Bernardine Dohrn. 2001. *Zero Tolerance: Resisting the Drive for Punishment in our Schools.* New York: The Free Press.

Band, Stephen R., and Joseph A. Harpold. 1999. "School Violence: Lessons Learned." *FBI Law Enforcement Bulletin.* 68: 9–16.

Bayles, Michael D. 1982. "Punishment for Attempts." *Social Theory and Practice* 8: 21–29.

Beck, Ulrich. 1992. *The Risk Society: Towards a New Modernity.* London: Sage.

Becker, Lawrence C. 1973/74. "Criminal Attempt and the Theory of the Law of Crimes." *Philosophy & Public Affairs* 3: 262–294.

Bell, Emma. 2011. *Criminal Justice and Neoliberalism.* Basingstoke: Palgrave Macmillan.

Bernstein, Arnie. 2009. *Bath Massacre: America's First School Bombing.* Ann Arbor, MI: University of Michigan Press.

Best, Joel. 2002. "Monster Hype." *Education Next.* 2: 51–55.

Borum, Randy. 2000. "Assessing Violence Risk among Youth." *Journal of Clinical Psychology* 56: 1263–1288.
Borum, Randy, Dewey Cornell, William Modzeleski, and Shane Jimerson. 2010. "What Can Be Done about School Shootings?: A Review of the Evidence." *Educational Researcher* 39(1): 27–37.
Bower, Amanda. 2001. "Scorecard of Hatred." *Time Magazine*. Retrieved August 3, 2010 (http://www.time.com/time/magazine/article/0,9171,999476,00.html).
Brady Center to Prevent Gun Violence. (n.d.). "Major School Shootings in the United States Since 1997." Washington, D.C. Retrieved July 15, 2010 (http://www.bradycampaign.org/xshare/pdf/school-shootings.pdf).
Brady, Kevin P., Sharon Balmer, and Deinya Phenix. 2007. "School-Police Partnership Effectiveness in Urban Schools." *Education and Urban Society* 39: 455–478.
Brank, Eve M., Jennifer L. Woolard, Veda E. Brown, Mark Fondacaro, Jennifer L. Luescher, Ramona G. Chinn, and Scott A. Miller. 2007. "Will They Tell? Weapons Reporting by Middle-School Youth." *Youth Violence and Juvenile Justice* 5(2): 125–146.
Brinkley, Christy J., and David A. Saarnio. 2006. "Involving Students in School Violence Prevention: Are They Willing To Help? *Journal of School Violence* 5: 93–116.
Brint, Steven. 1998. *Schools and Societies*. Thousand Oaks: Pine Forge Press.
Burgess, Ann, Christina Garbarino, and Mary Carlson. 2006. "Pathological Teasing and Bullying Turned Deadly: Shooters and Suicide." *Victims & Offenders* 1: 1–13.
Burns, Ronald, and Charles Crawford. 1999. "School Shootings, the Media, and Public Fear: Ingredients for a Moral Panic." *Crime, Law & Social Change* 32: 147–168.
Butterfield, Fox with Robert McFadden. November 26, 2001. "3 Teenagers Held in Plot at Massachusetts School." Retrieved May 13, 2012 (http://www.nytimes.com/2001/11/26/us/3-teenagers-held-in-plot-at-massachusetts-school.html).
Campbell, Susan B. 1991. "Longitudinal Studies of Active and Aggressive Preschoolers: Individual Differences in Early Behavior and in Outcome." Pp. 57–90 in *Internalizing and Externalizing Expressions of Dysfunction: Volume 2 (Rochester Symposium on Developmental Psychopathology)*, edited by Dante Cicchetti and Sheree L. Toth. Hillsdale, NJ: Lawrence Erlbaum Associates, Inc.

Campbell, Susan B., Anna M. Breaux, Linda J. Ewing, and Emily K. Szumowski. 1986. "Correlates and Predictors of Hyperactivity and Aggression: A Longitudinal Study of Parent-Referred Problem Preschoolers." *Journal of Abnormal Child Psychology* 14: 217–234.

Canter, David and Donna Youngs. 2009. *Investigative Psychology: Offender Profiling and the Analysis of Criminal Action*. New York: Wiley.

Carter, Helen. September 2, 2009. "Manchester Teenagers Planned Columbine-Style Attack, Jury Told." Retrieved May 8, 2012 (http://www.guardian.co.uk/uk/2009/sep/02/manchester-teenagers-columbine-style-attack).

Casella, Ronnie. 2001. *Being Down: Challenging Violence in Urban Schools*. New York: Teachers College Press.

Casella, Ronnie. 2003. "The False Allure of Security Technologies." *Social Justice* 30(3): 82–93.

Casella, Ronnie. 2006. *Selling Us the Fortress: The Promotion of Techno-Security Equipment for Schools*. New York: Routledge.

Charmaz, Kathy C. 2001. "Grounded Theory." Pp. 335–352 in *Contemporary Field Research: Perspectives and Formulations*, edited by R.M. Emerson. Prospect Heights, IL: Waveland Press.

Christopher, Russell. 2004. "Does Attempted Murder Deserve Greater Punishment than Murder? Moral Luck and the Duty to Prevent Harm." *Notre Dame Journal of Law, Ethics, and Public Policy* 18(2): 419–435.

Civil Rights Data Collection. 2012. "U.S. Dept. of Education Office for Civil Rights." Retrieved May 26, 2013 (http://www2.ed.gov/about/offices/list/ocr/docs/crdc-2012-data-summary.pdf).

Clarke, Ronald V. 1995. "Situational Crime Prevention." *Crime and Justice* 19: 91–150.

Clear, Todd. 1994. *Harm in American Penology: Offenders, Victims, and Their Communities*. Albany, NY: SUNY Press.

Cohen, Stanley. 2002. *Folk Devils and Moral Panics: The Creation of the Mods and Rockers*. New York: Routledge.

Coleman, Loren. 2004. *The Copycat Effect: How the Media and Popular Culture Trigger the Mayhem in Tomorrow's Headlines*. New York: Simon and Schuster.

Collier, Richard. 1998. *Masculinities, Crime, and Criminology: Men, Heterosexuality, and the Criminal(ised) Other*. Thousand Oaks, CA: Sage.

Consalvo, Mia. 2003. "The Monsters Next Door: Media Constructions of Boys and Masculinity." *Feminist Media Studies* 3(1): 27–45.

Cornell, Dewey G. 2003. "Guidelines for Responding to Student Threats of Violence." *Journal of Educational Administration* 41: 705–719.

Cornell, Dewey G. 2006. *School Violence: Fear versus Facts*. Mahwah, NJ: Lawrence Erlbaum.

Cornell, Dewey G. 2013. "The Virginia Student Threat Assessment Guidelines: An Empirically Supported Violence Prevention Strategy." Pp. 379–400 in *School Shootings: International Research, Case Studies, and Concepts for Prevention*, edited by Nils Böckler, Wilhelm Heitmeyer, Peter Sitzer, and Thorsten Seeger. New York, N.Y.: Springer.

Cornell, Dewey G., and Peter L. Sheras. 2006. *Guidelines for Responding to Student Threats of Violence*. Longmont, CO: Sopris West.

Cornell, Dewey G., Peter L. Sheras, Sebastian Kaplan, David McConville, Julea Douglass, Andrea Elkon, Lela McKnight, Chris Branson, and Joanna Cole. 2004. "Guidelines for Student Threat Assessment: Field-Test Findings." *School Psychology Review* 33(4): 527–546.

Cramer, Clayton. 1995. "Ethical Problems of Mass Murder Coverage in the Mass Media." *Journal on Firearms and Public Policy* 7: 113–134.

Cullen, Dave. 2009. *Columbine*. New York: Twelve.

Culley, Marci R., Martha Conkling, James Emshoff, Craig Blakely, and Dennis Gorman. 2006. "Environmental and Contextual Influences on School Violence and its Prevention." *The Journal of Primary Prevention* 27(3): 217–227.

Daniels, Jeffrey A., Ilene Buck, Susan Croxall, Julia Gruber, Peter Kime and Heidi Govert. 2007. "A Content Analysis of News Reports of Averted School Rampages." *Journal of School Violence* 6: 83–99.

Daniels, Jeffrey A., Adam Volungis, Erin Pshenishny, Punita Gandhi, Amy Winkler, Daniel Cramer, and Mary Bradley. 2010. "A Qualitative Investigation of Averted School Shooting Rampages." *The Counseling Psychologist* 38(1): 69–95.

Daniels, Jeffrey A., and Mary C. Bradley. 2011. *Preventing Lethal School Violence*. New York, NY: Springer.

Davis, Michael. 1986. "Why Attempts Deserve Less Punishment than Complete Crimes." *Law and Philosophy* 5(1): 1–32.

Deisinger, Gene, Marisa Randazzo, Daniel O'Neill, and Jenna Savage. 2008. *The Handbook for Campus Threat Assessment and Management Teams*. Stoneham, MA: Applied Risk Management, LLC.

References

Denzin, Norman K. 1983. "Interpretive Interactionism." Pp. 129–146 in *Beyond Method: Strategies for Social Research*, edited by G. Morgan. Beverly Hills, CA: Sage.

Denzin, Norman K., and Yvonna S. Lincon. 2005. *The Sage Handbook of Qualitative Research*. Thousand Oaks, CA: Sage.

Dinkes, Rachel, Jana Kemp, Katrina Baum, and Thomas D. Snyder. 2009. Indicators of School Crime and Safety: 2009. (NCES 2010-012/NCJ 228478). National Center for Education Statistics, Institute of Education Sciences, U.S. Department of Education, and Bureau of Justice Statistics, Office of Justice Programs, U.S. Department of Justice. Washington, DC.

Douglas, John E., Robert K. Ressler, Ann W. Burgess, and Carol R. Hartman. 1986. "Criminal Profiling from Crime Scene Analysis." *Behavioral Sciences and the Law* 4: 401–421.

Duff, Antony. 1997. *Criminal Attempts*. Oxford: Oxford University Press.

Duwe, Grant. 2000. "Body-Count Journalism: The Presentation of Mass Murder in the News Media." *Homicide Studies* 4(4): 364–399.

Duwe, Grant. 2004. "The Patterns and Prevalence of Mass Murder in Twentieth-Century America." *Justice Quarterly* 21(4): 729–761.

Duwe, Grant. 2007. *Mass Murder in the United States: A History*. Jefferson, NC: McFarland & Company, Inc.

Dwyer, Kevin P., David Osher, and Cynthia Warger. 1998. "Early Warning, Timely Response: A Guide to Safe Schools." Washington, DC: U.S. Department of Education.

Eliot, Megan, Dewey Cornell, Anne Gregory, and Xitao Fan. 2010. "Supportive School Climate and Student Willingness to Seek Help for Bullying and Threats of Violence. *Journal of School Psychology* 48(6): 533–553.

Enker, Arnold N. 1977. "Mens Rea and Criminal Attempt." *Law & Social Inquiry* 2(4): 845–879.

Epstein, Joel. 2002. "Breaking the Code of Silence: Bystanders to Campus Violence and the Law of College and University Safety." *Stetson Law Review* 32: 91–124.

Farrington, David P. 1991. "Childhood Aggression and Adult Violence: Early Precursors and Later-life Outcomes." Pp. 5–29 in *The Development and Treatment of Childhood Aggression*, edited by Debra J. Pepler and Kenneth H. Rubin. Hillsdale, NJ: Lawrence Erlbaum Associates, Inc.

Feeley, Malcolm, and Jonathan Simon. 1992. 'The New Penology: Notes on the Emerging Strategy of Corrections and its Implications." *Criminology* 30(4): 449–470.
Feeley, Malcolm, and Jonathan Simon. 1994. "Actuarial Justice: The Emerging New Criminal Law." Pp. 173–201 in *The Futures of Criminology*, edited by David Nelken. London: Sage.
Fein, Robert A., Bryan Vossekuil, and Gwen Holden. 1995. "Threat Assessment: An Approach to Prevent Targeted Violence." Pp. 1–7 in *National Institute of Justice: Research in Action*. U.S. Department of Justice, Office of Justice Programs. Washington, D.C.
Fein, Robert A., Bryan Vossekuil, William Pollack, Randy Borum, William Modzeleski, and Marisa Reddy. 2002. *Threat Assessment in Schools: A Guide to Managing Threatening Situations and to Creating Safe School Climates*. U.S. Department of Education, Office of Elementary and Secondary Education, Safe and Drug-Free Schools Program and U.S. Secret Service, National Threat Assessment Center. Washington, D.C.
Feinberg, Joel. 1995. "Equal Punishment for Failed Attempts: Some Bad but Instructive Arguments against It." *Arizona Law Review* 37: 117–133.
Felson, Marcus. 1994. *Crime and Everyday Life: Insight and Implications for Society*. Thousand Oaks, CA: Pine Forge.
Fenning, Pamela and Jennifer Rose. 2007. "Overrepresentation of African American Students in Exclusionary Discipline: The Role of School Policy." *Urban Education* 42(6): 536–559.
Flegenheimer, Matt. 2013. "Final Report on Sandy Hook Killings Sheds New Light on Gunman's Isolation." *The New York Times*. Retrieved February 1, 2014 (http://www.nytimes.com/2013/12/28/nyregion/with-release-of-final-sandy-hook-shooting-report-investigation-is-said-to-be-over.html?pagewanted=1&_r=1&).
Foucault, Michel. 1977. *Discipline and Punish: The Birth of the Prison*. Harmondsworth: Penguin.
Foucault, Michel. 1980. *Power/Knowledge*. Brighton, UK: Harvester.
Foucault, Michel. 1991. "Governmentality." Pp. 87–104 in *The Foucault Effect: Studies in Governmentality*, edited by Graham Burchell, Colin Gordon and Peter Miller. London, UK: Harvester Wheatsheaf.
Foucault, Michel. 2009. *Security, Territory, Population: Lectures at the Collège de France 1977–1978*. New York: Palgrave Macmillan.

References

Fox, James Alan, and Jack Levin. 1994. *Overkill: Mass Murder and Serial Killing Exposed*. New York: Plenum Press.

Fox, James Alan, and Jack Levin. 1998. "Multiple Homicide: Patterns of Serial and Mass Murder." *Crime and Justice* 23: 407–455.

Fox, James Alan, Jack Levin, and Kenna Quinet. 2005. *The Will to Kill: Making Sense of Senseless Murder*, 2nd Edition. Boston, MA: Allyn and Bacon.

Fox, James Alan, and Jenna Savage. 2009. "Mass Murder Goes to College: An Examination of Changes on College Campuses Following Virginia Tech. *American Behavioral Scientist* 52(10): 1286–1308.

Fox, James Alan, and Harvey Burstein. 2010. *Violence and Security on Campus: From Preschool through College*. Santa Barbara, CA: Praeger.

Fox, James Alan, and Jack Levin. 2011. *Extreme Killing: Understanding Serial and Mass Murder*. Thousand Oaks, CA: Sage.

Garland, David. 2001. *The Culture of Control: Crime and Social Order in Contemporary Society*. Chicago: University of Chicago Press.

Gaughan, Edward, Jay D. Cerio, and Robert A. Myers. 2001. *Lethal Violence in Schools: A National Survey*. Alfred, NY: Alfred University.

Giddens, Anthony. 1999. "Risk and Responsibility." *The Modern Law Review* 62(1): 1–10.

Glassner, Barry. 2010. *The Culture of Fear: Why Americans Are Afraid of the Wrong Things, Tenth Anniversary Edition*. New York: Basic Books.

Glaser, Barney G., and Anselm L. Strauss. 1967. *The Discovery of Grounded Theory: Strategies for Qualitative Research*. Chicago, IL: Aldine.

Goldson, Barry. 2002. "New Punitiveness: The Politics of Child Incarceration." Pp. 386–400 in *Youth Justice: Critical Readings*, edited by John Muncie, Gordon Hughes, and Eugene McLaughlin. London: Sage.

Goodrich, Juliette. April 11, 2012. "Accused Gunman in Oakland Massacre Tells CBS 5 He's 'Deeply Sorry.'" Retrieved April 13, 2012 (http://sanfrancisco.cbslocal.com/2012/04/11/exclusive-jailhouse-interview-accused-gunman-in-oakland-massacre-talks-to-cbs-5/).

Gottesdiener, Laura. April 21, 2011. "After Arizona Veto, Guns on Campus Legislation Still Pending in Other States." Retrieved April 5, 2014 (http://www.huffingtonpost.com/2011/04/21/guns-on-campus_n_851814.html).

Grisso, Thomas. 2009. "Forward." Pp. xv–xvii in *Handbook of Violence Risk Assessment and Treatment: New Approaches for Mental Health Professionals*, edited by Joel T. Andrade. New York, NY: Springer.

Grubin, Don and Sarah Wingate. 1996. "Sexual Offence Recidivism: Prediction versus Understanding." *Criminal Behaviour and Mental Health* 6: 349–359.

Guba, Egon. 1981. "Criteria for Assessing the Trustworthiness of Naturalistic Inquiry." *Educational Communication and Technology Journal* 29(2): 75–91.

Guba, Egon, and Yvonna Lincoln. 1982. "Epistemological and Methodological Bases of Naturalistic Inquiry." *Educational Communication and Technology Journal* 30: 233–252.

Haenfler, Ross. 2009. *Goths, Gamers, and Grrrls: Deviance and Youth Subcultures*. Oxford: Oxford University Press.

Hagan, John, Paul Hirschfeld, and Carla Shedd. 2002. "First and Last Words: Apprehending the Social and Legal Facts of an Urban High School Shooting." *Sociological Methods and Research* 31(2): 218–255.

Haider-Markel, Donald P., and Mark R. Joslyn. 2001. "Gun Policy, Opinion, Tragedy, and Blame Attribution: The Conditional Influence of Issue Frames." *Journal of Politics* 63: 520–543.

Halbig, Wolfgang W. 2000. "Breaking the Code of Silence." *American School Board Journal* 187(3): 34–36.

Harcourt, Bernard. 2007. *Against Prediction: Profiling, Policing, and Punishing in an Actuarial Age*. Chicago, IL: University of Chicago Press.

Harcourt, Bernard. 2010. "Neoliberal Penality: A Brief Genealogy." *Theoretical Criminology* 14(1): 74–92.

Harding, David, Cybelle Fox, and Jal D. Mehta. 2002. "Studying Rare Events through Qualitative Case Studies: Lessons from a Study of Rampage School Shootings." *Sociological Methods and Research* 31(2): 174–217.

Henry, Stuart. 2009. "School Violence Beyond Columbine: A Complex Problem in Need of an Interdisciplinary Analysis." *American Behavioral Scientist* 52(9): 1246–1265.

Hirschfield, Paul J. 2008. "Preparing for Prison? The Criminalization of School Discipline in the USA." *Theoretical Criminology* 12(1): 79–101.

Hirschfield, Paul J. 2010. "School Surveillance in America: Disparate and Unequal." Pp. 38–54 in *Schools under Surveillance: Cultures of*

Control in Public Education, edited by Torin Monahan and Rodolfo D. Torress. New Brunswick, NJ: Rutgers University Press.

Hirschfield, Paul J., and Katarzyna Celinska. 2011. "Beyond Fear: Sociological Perspectives on the Criminalization of School Discipline." *Sociology Compass* 5(1): 1–12.

Holcomb, Alison, and Michael J. Allen. December 9, 2009. "Moving beyond Zero Tolerance." American Civil Liberties Union of Washington. Retrieved September 20, 2010 (http://www.aclu-wa.org/news/moving-beyond-zero-tolerance).

Holmes, Ronald M., and Stephen T. Holmes. 2001. *Mass Murder in the United States*. Upper Saddle River, NJ: Prentice Hall.

Homant, Robert J., and Daniel B. Kennedy. 1998. "Psychological Aspects of Crime Scene Profiling: Validity Research." *Criminal Justice and Behavior* 25: 319–343.

Hong, Jun Sung, Hyunkag Cho, Paula Allen-Meares, and Dorothy L. Espelage. 2011. "The Social Ecology of the Columbine High School Shootings." *Children and Youth Services Review* 33: 861–868.

Hymowitz, Kay S. April 18, 2005. "Zero Tolerance Policies Are Necessary to Prevent School Violence." Pp. 24–26 in *How Can School Violence Be Prevented?*, edited by Scott Barbour. New York: Thomson-Gale.

International Association of Chiefs of Police. 1999. *Guidelines for Preventing and Responding to School Violence*. Alexandria, VA.

Irigaray, Luce [translated by Catherine Porter and Carolyn Burke]. 1985. *This Sex Which Is Not One*. New York: Cornell University Press.

James, Susan Donaldson. April 13, 2009. "Columbine Shootings 10 Years Later: Students, Teacher Still Haunted by Post-Traumatic Stress." *ABC News*. Retrieved September 20, 2010 (http://abcnews.go.com/Health/story?id=7300782&page=1).

Jimerson, Shane R., Stephen E. Brock, and Katherine Cowan. 2005. "Threat Assessment: An Essential Component of a Comprehensive Safe School Program." *Principal Leadership* 6(2): 11–15.

Karp, David R., and Beau Breslin. 2001. "Restorative Justice in School Communities." *Youth & Society* 33(2): 249–272.

Keppel, Robert D. 2006. *Offender Profiling*. Mason, OH: Thomson Custom Publishing.

Kiefer, Heather Mason. 2005. "Public: Society Powerless to Stop School Shootings." Retrieved March 1, 2014 (http://www.gallup.com/poll/15511/Public-Society-Powerless-Stop-School-Shootings.aspx).

Kim, Catherine, Daniel Losen, and Damon Hewitt. 2010. *The School-to-Prison Pipeline: Structuring Legal Reform*. New York: New York University Press.

Kimmel, Michael S., and Matthew Mahler. 2003. "Adolescent Masculinity, Homophobia, and Violence." *American Behavioral Scientist* 46: 1439–1458.

Klein, Jessie. 2005. "Teaching Her a Lesson: Media Misses Boys' Rage Relating to Girls in School Shootings." *Crime, Media, Culture* 1(1): 90–97.

Klein, Jessie. 2012. *The Bully Society: School Shootings and the Crisis of Bullying in American Schools*. New York: NYU Press.

Kleinman, Sherryl, Martha Copp, and Karla Henderson. 1997. "Qualitatively Different: Teaching Fieldwork to Graduate Students." *Journal of Contemporary Ethnography* 25: 469–499.

Kocsis, Richard N. 2007. *Criminal Profiling: International Theory, Research, and Practice*. Totowa, NJ: Humana Press.

Kocsis, Richard N., Harvey J. Irwin, Andrew F. Hayes, and Ronald Nunn. 2000. "Expertise in Psychological Profiling: A Comparative Assessment." *Journal of Interpersonal Violence* 15(3): 311–331.

Kohn, Alfie. 2004. "Rebuilding School Culture to Make Schools Safer." *The Education Digest* 70(3): 23–30.

Kupchik, Aaron. 2010. *Homeroom Security: School Discipline in an Age of Fear*. New York: New York University Press.

Kupchik, Aaron, and Torin Monahan. 2006. "The New American School: Preparation for Post-Industrial Discipline." *British Journal of Sociology of Education* 27(5): 617–631.

Langman, Peter. 2005. "Can School Shootings be Prevented?" *Healing Magazine* 10(2): 24–27. Retrieved September 14, 2010 (http://www.kidspeace.org/uploadedFiles/SchoolShooting_Langman.pdf).

Langman, Peter. 2009a. *Why Kids Kill: Inside the Minds of School Shooters*. New York: Palgrave Macmillan.

Langman, Peter. 2009b. "Rampage School Shooters: A Typology." *Aggression and Violent Behavior* 14(1): 79–86.

Larkin, Ralph W. 2007. *Comprehending Columbine*. Philadelphia, PA: Temple University Press.

Larkin, Ralph W. 2009. "The Columbine Legacy: Rampage Shootings as Political Acts." *American Behavioral Scientist* 52(9): 1309–1326.

Latané, Bibb, and John M. Darley. 1969. "Bystander 'Apathy.'" *American Scientist* 57: 244–268.

Lawrence, Regina G., and Thomas A. Birkland. 2004. "Guns, Hollywood, and School Safety: Defining the School-Shooting Problem across the Public Arenas." *Social Science Quarterly* 85: 1193–1207.

Lawrence, Richard. 2007. *School Crime and Juvenile Justice*. New York, NY: Oxford University Press.

Leary, Mark R., Robin M. Kowalski, Laura Smith and Stephen Phillips. 2003. "Teasing, Rejection, and Violence: Case Studies of the School Shootings." *Aggressive Behavior* 29: 202–214.

Leitsinger, Miranda. March 8, 2012. "When Rumor, the Internet and School Violence Fears Collide." Retrieved May 4, 2012 (http://usnews.msnbc.msn.com/_news/2012/03/08/10604539-when-rumor-the-internet-and-school-violence-fears-collide?lite).

Levin, Jack, and Eric Madfis. 2009. "Mass Murder at School and Cumulative Strain: A Sequential Model." *American Behavioral Scientist* 52(9): 1227–1245.

Levin, Jack, and James Alan Fox. 1999. "Making Sense of Mass Murder." Pp. 173–187 in *Handbook of Psychological Approaches with Violent Offenders: Contemporary Strategies and Issues*, edited by Vincent B. Van Hasselt and Michel Hersen. Norwell, MA: Kluwer Academic.

Lickel, Brian, Toni Schmader, and David Hamilton. 2003. "A Case of Collective Responsibility: Who Else Was to Blame for the Columbine High School Shootings?" *Personality & Social Psychology Bulletin* 29: 194–204.

Lieberman, Joseph A. 2008. *School Shootings: What Every Parent and Educator Needs to Know to Protect Our Children*. New York: Citadel Press.

Lincoln, Yvonna, and Egon Guba. 1985. *Naturalistic Inquiry*. Beverly Hills, CA: Sage

Lintott, Joseph. 2004. "Teaching and Learning in the Face of School Violence. *Georgetown Journal on Poverty Law & Policy* 11(3): 553–580.

"List of School-Related Attacks – Foiled or Exposed Plots." No Date. Retrieved July 15, 2010 (http://en.wikipedia.org/wiki/List_of_school-related_attacks#Foiled_or_exposed_plots).

Lodge, Jodie, and Erica Frydenberg. 2005. "The Role of Peer Bystanders in School Bullying: Positive Steps toward Promoting Peaceful Schools." *Theory into Practice* 44(4): 329–336.

Logan, Casey. May 2, 2002. "Columbine Jitters May Cost a Kansas Town Millions." *The Pitch*. Retrieved July 15, 2010 (http://www.pitch.com/2002-05-02/news/tutu-careful/).

Lyons, William, and Julie Drew. 2006. *Punishing Schools: Fear and Citizenship in American Public Education*. Ann Arbor, MI: University of Michigan Press.

MacDonald, Irene M., and Jose L. da Costa. 1996. "Exploring Issues of School Violence: The 'Code of Silence.'" Paper presented at the conference of the Canadian Association for the Study of Educational Administration, St. Catherines, Ontario, Canada.

Madfis, Eric. 2014a (in press). "Averting School Rampage: Student Intervention Amid a Persistent Code of Silence." *Youth Violence and Juvenile Justice*.

Madfis, Eric. 2014b. "Triple Entitlement and Homicidal Anger: An Exploration of the Intersectional Identities of American Mass Murderers." *Men and Masculinities* 17(1): 67–86.

Madfis, Eric, and Jack Levin. 2013. "School Rampage in International Perspective: The Salience of Cumulative Strain Theory." Pp. 79–104 in *School Shootings: International Research, Case Studies, and Concepts for Prevention*, edited by Nils Böckler, Wilhelm Heitmeyer, Peter Sitzer, and Thorsten Seeger. New York, NY: Springer.

Mai, Rebecca, and Judith Alpert. 2000. "Separation and Socialization: A Feminist Analysis of the School Shootings at Columbine." *Journal for the Psychoanalysis of Culture and Society* 5: 264–275.

Mathes, Eugene W., and Arnold Kahn. 1975. "Diffusion of Responsibility and Extreme Behavior." *Journal of Personality and Social Psychology* 31(5): 881–886.

McCabe, Kimberly A., and Gregory M. Martin. 2005. *School Violence, the Media, and Criminal Justice Responses*. New York: Lang.

McCluskey, Gillean, Gwynedd Lloyd, Jean Kane, Sheila Riddell, Joan Stead and Elisabet Weedon. 2008. "Can Restorative Practices in Schools Make a Difference?" *Educational Review*. 60(4): 405–417.

McCrimmon, Katie Kerwin. 2009. "The Story of Safe2Tell." Denver, CO: The Colorado Trust. Retrieved May 23, 2012 (http://safe2tell.org/wp-content/uploads/2009/03/storys2t.pdf).

McGee, James P., and Caren R. DeBernardo. 1999. "The Classroom Avenger: A Behavioral Profile of School Based Shootings." *The Forensic Examiner* 8: 16–18.

McMillin, Sue. April 18, 2009. "Getting Teens to Talk May Be Key to Secure Schools." Retrieved May 23, 2012 (http://www.gazette.com/entertainment/school-51999-teen-schools.html).

Meloy, J. Reid, Anthony G. Hempel, Kris Mohandie, Andrew A. Shiva, and B. Thomas Gray. 2001. "Offender and Offense Characteristics of a Nonrandom Sample of Adolescent Mass Murders." *Journal of the American Academy of Child and Adolescent Psychiatry* 40(6): 719–728.

Meloy, J. Reid, Anthony G. Hempel, B. Thomas Gray, Kris Mohandie, Andrew A. Shiva, and T.C. Richards. 2004. "A Comparative Analysis of North American Adolescent and Adult Mass Murderers." *Behavioral Sciences and the Law* 22(3): 291–309.

Meloy, J. Reid, and Mary Ellen O'Toole. 2011. "The Concept of Leakage in Threat Assessment." *Behavioral Sciences and the Law* 29: 513–527.

Menninger, Karl. 1968. *The Crime of Punishment*. New York: Penguin Books.

Merida, Kevin. April 27, 1999. "Fearful Kids Maintain Code of Silence." *Washington Post*. Retrieved October 3, 2010 (http://www.washingtonpost.com/wp-srv/national/daily/april99/snitch042799.htm).

Messerschmidt, James W. 1993. *Masculinities and Crime: Critique and Reconceptualization of Theory*. New York: Rowan & Littlefield.

Meyer, Luanna H., and Ian M. Evans. 2012. *The Teacher's Guide to Restorative Classroom Discipline*. Thousand Oaks, CA: Sage.

Mirsky, Laura. 2003. "Safer SanerSchools: Transforming School Culture with Restorative Practices." International Institute for Restorative Practices. Retrieved February 18, 2014 (http://www.iirp.edu/iirpWebsites/web/uploads/article_pdfs/ssspilots.pdf).

Moeller, Thomas G. 2001. *Youth Aggression and Violence: A Psychological Approach*. Mahwah, NJ: Lawrence Erlbaum Associates, Inc.

Monahan, Torin, and Rodolfo D. Torres (Editors). 2010. *Schools under Surveillance: Cultures of Control in Public Education*. New Brunswick, NJ: Rutgers University Press.

Moore, Mark H., Carol V. Petrie, Anthony A. Braga, and Brenda L. McLaughlin. 2003. *Deadly Lessons: Understanding Lethal School Violence*. Washington, DC: National Academies Press.

Morris, Edward W. 2010. "'Snitches End Up in Ditches' and Other Cautionary Tales." *Journal of Contemporary Criminal Justice* 26(3): 254–272.

Morrison, Brenda. (2007). *Restoring Safe School Communities: A Whole School Response to Bullying, Violence and Alienation.* Sidney, Australia: Federation Press.

Mossman, Douglas. 1994. "Assessing Predictions of Violence: Being Accurate about Accuracy." *Journal of Consulting and Clinical Psychology* 62: 783–792.

Mossman, Douglas. 2006. "Critique of Pure Risk Assessment or, Kant Meets Tarasoff." *University of Cincinnati Law Review* 75: 523–609.

Mullen, Paul E. 2004. "The Autogenic (Self-Generated) Massacre." *Behavioral Sciences and the Law* 22: 311–323.

Muncie, John. 2008. "The 'Punitive Turn' in Juvenile Justice: Cultures of Control and Rights Compliance in Western Europe and the USA." *Youth Justice* 8(2): 107–121.

Muschert, Glenn W. 2007. "Research in School Shootings." *Sociology Compass* 1(1): 60–80.

Muschert, Glenn W., and Anthony A. Peguero. 2010. "The Columbine Effect and School Anti-Violence Policy." *Research in Social Problems and Public Policy* 17: 117–148.

Muschert, Glenn W., and Massimo Ragnedda. 2010. "Media and Control of Violence: Communication in School Shootings." Pp. 345–361 in *Control of Violence: Historical and International Perspectives on Violence in Modern Societies*, edited by Wilhelm Heitmeyer, Heinz-Gerhard Haupt, Andrea Kirschner, and Stefan Malthaner. New York: Springer Publishing.

Muschert, Glenn W., and Eric Madfis. 2013. "Fear of School Violence in the Post-Columbine Era." Pp. 13–34 in *Responding to School Violence: Confronting the Columbine Effect*, edited by Glenn W. Muschert, Stuart Henry, Nicole L. Bracy, and Anthony A. Peguero. Boulder, CO: Lynne Rienner Publishers.

Muschert, Glenn W., Stuart Henry, Nicole L. Bracy, and Anthony A. Peguero (Editors). 2013. *Responding to School Violence: Confronting the Columbine Effect.* Boulder, CO: Lynne Rienner Publishers.

Muzzatti, Stephen L. 2004. "Criminalising Marginality and Resistance: Marilyn Manson, Columbine, and Cultural Criminology." Pp. 143–154 in *Cultural Criminology Unleased*, edited by Jeff Ferrell, Keith Hayward, Wayne Morrison, and Mike Presdee. London: Glasshouse Press.

Mythen, Gabe. 2008. "Sociology and the Art of Risk." *Sociology Compass* 2(1): 299–316.

Neroni, Hilary. 2000. "The Men of Columbine: Violence and Masculinity in American Culture and Film." *Journal for the Psychoanalysis of Culture and Society* 5: 256–263.

Newman, Katherine S., Cybelle Fox, Wendy Roth, Jal Mehta, and David Harding. 2004. *Rampage: The Social Roots of School Shooters*. New York: Perseus Books Group.

Newman, Katherine S., and Cybelle Fox. 2009. "Repeat Tragedy: Rampage Shootings in American High School and College Settings, 2002–2008." *American Behavioral Scientist* 52(9): 1286–1308.

Noguera, Pedro A. 1995. "Preventing and Producing Violence: A Critical Analysis of Responses to School Violence." *Harvard Education Review* 65(2): 189–212.

Nolan, Kathleen. 2011. *Police in the Hallways: Discipline in an Urban School*. Minneapolis: University of Minnesota Press.

Ogle, Jennifer Paff, Molly Eckman, and Catherine Amoroso Leslie. 2003. "Appearance Cues and the Shootings at Columbine High: Construction of a Social Problem in the Print Media." *Sociological Inquiry* 73(1): 1–27.

Ohana, Daniel. 2007. "Desert and Punishment for Acts Preparatory to the Commission of a Crime." *Canadian Journal of Law and Jurisprudence* 20: 113–142.

O'Malley, Pat. 2008. "Neoliberalism and Risk in Criminology." Pp. 55–67 in *The Critical Criminology Companion*, edited by Thalia Anthony and Chris Cunneen. Sydney, Australia: Federation Press,

O'Toole, Mary E. 2000. "The School Shooter: A Threat Assessment Perspective." Critical Incident Response Group, National Center for the Analysis of Violent Crime, FBI Academy, Quantico, Virginia. Retrieved September 30, 2010 (http://www.fbi.gov/stats-services/publications/school-shooter).

Otto, Randy K. 2000. "Assessing and Managing Violence Risk in Outpatient Settings." *Journal of Clinical Psychology* 56: 1239–1262.

Palermo, George B., and Lee E. Ross. 1999. "Mass Murder, Suicide, and Moral Development: Can We Separate the Adults from the Juveniles?" *International Journal of Offender Therapy and Comparative Criminology* 43(1): 8–20.

Palermo, George B., and Richard N. Kocsis. 2005. *Offender Profiling: An Introduction to the Sociopsychological Analysis Of Violent Crime*. Springfield, IL: Charles C. Thomas Publisher.

Pattillo, Mary, David Weiman, and Bruce Western. 2004. *Imprisoning America: The Social Effects of Mass Incarceration*. Russell Sage Foundation Publications.

Payne, Susan R. T., and Delbert S. Elliott. 2011. "Safe2Tell: An Anonymous, 24/7 Reporting System for Preventing School Violence." *New Directions in Youth Development* 129: 103–111.

Perez, Steve. March 5, 2011. "Where is the Santana Shooter Now?" Retrieved April 13, 2012 (http://santee.patch.com/articles/where-is-the-santana-shooter-now).

Petherick, Wayne. 2006. *Serial Crime: Theoretical and Practical Issues in Behavioral Profiling*. Burlington, MA: Academic Press.

Petee, Thomas A., Kathy G. Padgett, and Thomas S. York. 1997. "Debunking the Stereotype: An Examination of Mass Murder in Public Places." *Homicide Studies* 1(4): 317–337.

Pinizzotto, Anthony, and Norman J. Finkel. 1990. "Criminal Personality Profiling: An Outcome and Process Study." *Law & Human Behavior* 14: 215–233.

Pollack, William S., William Modzeleski, and Georgeann Rooney. 2008. "Prior Knowledge of Potential School-Based Violence: Information Students Learn May Prevent a Targeted Attack." United States Secret Service and United States Department of Education. Washington D.C.

Pratt, John, David Brown, Mark Brown, Simon Hallsworth, and Wayne Morrison. 2005. *The New Punitiveness: Trends, Theories, Perspectives*. Portland: Willan Publishing.

Public Agenda. 2004. *Teaching Interrupted: Do Discipline Policies in Today's Public Schools Foster the Common Good?* New York: Public Agenda. Retrieved April 13, 2012 (http://www.publicagenda.org/files/pdf/teaching_interrupted.pdf).

Randazzo, Marisa Reddy, Randy Borum, Bryan Vossekuil, Robert Fein, William Modzeleski, and William Pollack. 2006. "Threat Assessment in Schools: Empirical Support and Comparison with Other Approaches." Pp. 147–156 in *The Handbook of School Violence and School Safety: From Research to Practice*, edited by Shane R. Jimerson and Michael J. Furlong. Mahwah, NJ: Lawrence J. Erlbaum Associates.

Rappaport, Nancy, and James G. Barrett. 2009. "Under the Gun: Threat Assessment in Schools." *American Medical Association Journal of Ethics* 11(2): 149–154.

Reddy, Marissa, Randy Borum, John Berglund, Bryan Vossekuil, Robert Fein and William Modzeleski. 2001. "Evaluating Risk for Targeted Violence in Schools: Comparing Risk Assessment, Threat Assessment, and Other Approaches." *Psychology in the Schools* 38(2): 157–172.

Rigakos, George S., and Richard W. Hadden. 2001. "Crime, Capitalism and the 'Risk Society': Towards the Same Olde Modernity?" *Theoretical Criminology* 5(1): 61–84.

Robins, Lee N. 1966. *Deviant Children Grown Up: A Sociological and Psychiatric Study of Sociopathic Personality*. Baltimore, MD: The Williams & Wilkins Company.

Robbins, Christopher. 2005. "Zero Tolerance and the Politics of Racial Injustice." *The Journal of Negro Education* 74(1): 2–17.

Robertson, Tatsha. December 16, 2001. "Across the Nation, School Attack Plots Pose Legal Challenge." *Boston Globe*. Pp. A1, A26.

Rosenbaum, Dennis P., Arthur J. Lurigio, Robert C. Davis (Editors). 1998. *The Prevention of Crime: Social and Situational Strategies*. Belmont, CA: Wadsworth.

Rosenfeld, Richard, Bruce A. Jacobs, and Richard Wright. 2003. "Snitching and the Code of the Street." *British Journal of Criminology* 43: 291–309.

Ruddy, Sally A., Samantha Neiman, Cassie Hryczaniuk, Teresa L. Thomas, Randall J. Parmer, and Monica R. Hill. 2010. "2007–08 School Survey on Crime and Safety (SSOCS): Survey Documentation for Public-Use Data File Users." National Center for Education Statistics, Institute of Education Sciences, U.S. Department of Education. Washington, DC. Retrieved April 13, 2012 (http://nces.ed.gov/pubs2010/2010307.pdf).

Sacco, Frank C., and Reed Larsen. 2003. "Threat Assessment in Schools: A Critique of an Ongoing Intervention." *Journal of Applied Psychoanalytic Studies* 5(2): 171–188.

Sachsman, Susanne. September 8, 1997. "Prof Stalkers Beware: MOSAIC is Here." *Yale Daily News*.

Sanders, Clinton. 2004. "Forward." Pp. vii–xiii in *Brute Force: Animal Police and the Challenge of Cruelty*, by Arnold Arluke. West Lafayette, IN: Purdue University Press.

Schiele, Jerome H., and Ron Stewart. 2001. "When White Boys Kill: An Afrocentric Analysis." *Journal of Human Behavior in the Social Environment* 4(4): 253–273.

Schlafly, Phyllis. April 23, 2003. "Zero Tolerance or Zero Common Sense." *Eagle Forum*. Retrieved September 20, 2010 (http://www.eagleforum.org/column/2003/apr03/03-04-23.shtml).

Schofield, Janet W. 2002. "Increasing the Generalizability of Qualitative Research." Pp. 171–204 in *The Qualitative Researcher's Companion*, edited by A. Michael Huberman and Matthew B. Miles. Thousand Oaks, CA: Sage Publications.

Schutt, Russell K. 2004. *Investigating the Social World: The Process and Practice of Research*. Thousand Oaks: Pine Forge Press.

Schwarz, Eitan, and Janice Kowalski. 1991. "Malignant Memories: Posttraumatic Stress Disorder in Children and Adults Following a School Shooting." *Journal of the American Academy of Child and Adolescent Psychiatry* 30: 937–944.

Sewell, Kenneth W., and Michaela Mendelsohn. 2000. "Profiling Potentially Violent Youth: Statistical and Conceptual Problems." *Children's Services: Social Policy, Research, and Practice* 3(3): 147–169.

Shapiro, Jeremy, Rebekah L. Dorman, and William M. Burkey. 1997. "Development and Factor Analysis of a Measure of Youth Attitudes toward Guns and Violence. *Journal of Clinical Child Psychology* 26(3): 311–320.

Sherman, Lawrence, W., David P. Farrington, Brandon C. Welsh, and Doris L. MacKenzie (Editors). 2002. *Evidence-Based Crime Prevention*. New York: Routledge.

Sherman, Lawrence W., and Heather Strang. 2007. *Restorative Justice: The Evidence*. London: The Smith Institute.

Simon, Jonathan. 2006. *Governing Through Crime: How the War on Crime Transformed American Democracy and Created a Culture of Fear*. Oxford: Oxford University Press.

Skiba, Russell. 2000. "Zero Tolerance, Zero Evidence: An Analysis of School Disciplinary Practice." Policy Research Report. Indiana Education Policy Center.

Skiba, Russell, and Reece Peterson. 1999. "The Dark Side of Zero Tolerance: Can Punishment Lead to Safe Schools?" *Phi Delta Kappan* 80(5): 372–382.

Skiba, Russell, Robert S. Michael, Abra C. Nardo, and Reece L. Peterson. 2002. "The Color of Discipline: Source of Racial and Gender Disproportionality in School Punishment." *The Urban Review* 34(4): 317–342.

Spitalli, Samuel J. 2003. "Breaking the Code of Silence" *American School Board Journal* 190(9): 56–58.

Spjut, R. J. 1987. "When is an Attempt to Commit an Impossible Crime a Criminal Act." *Arizona Law Review* 29(2): 247–279.

Stancato, Frank A. 2001. "The Columbine Tragedy: Adolescent Identity and Future Recommendations." *The Clearing House* 77(1): 19–22.

Steiker, Carol S. 1998. "Forward: The Limits of the Preventive State." *Journal of Criminal Law & Criminology.* 88(3): 771–808.

Strong, Ken, and Dewey Cornell. 2008. "Student Threat Assessment in Memphis City Schools: A Descriptive Report." *Behavioral Disorders* 34: 42–54.

"Student Suspended After Finger Gun Incident." April 18, 2010. Abclocal.go.com. Retrieved October 3, 2010 (http://abclocal.go.com/ktrk/story?section=news/local&id=7392273).

Stueve, Ann, Kimberly Dash, Lydia O'Donnell, Parisa Tehranifar, Renee Wilson-Simmons, Ronald G. Slaby, and Bruce G. Link. 2006. "Rethinking the Bystander Role in School Violence Prevention." *Health Promotion Practice* 7(1):117–124.

Sulkowski, Michael L. 2011. "An Investigation of Students' Willingness to Report Threats of Violence in Campus Communities." *Psychology of Violence* 1(1): 53–65.

Sullivan, Mercer L., and Rob T. Guerette. 2003. "The Copycat Factor: Mental Illness, Guns, and The Shooting Incident at Heritage High School, Rockdale County, Georgia." Pp. 25–69 in *Deadly Lessons: Understanding Lethal School Violence*, edited by Mark H. Moore. Washington D.C.: National Academies Press.

Sumner, Michael D., Carol J. Silverman, and Mary Louise Frampton. 2010. "School-based Restorative Justice as an Alternative to Zero-Tolerance Policies: Lessons from West Oakland. Henderson Center for Social Justice. University of California, Berkeley, School of Law.

Syvertsen, Amy K., Constance A. Flanagan, and Michael D. Stout. 2009. "Code of Silence: Students' Perceptions of School Climate and Willingness to Intervene in a Peer's Dangerous Plan." *Journal of Educational Psychology* 101(1): 219–232.

Teicher, Stacy A. October 19, 2006. "How Students Can Break the 'Code of Silence': A Number of Resources Let Students Anonymously Voice Their Concerns about Troubling Issues at School. *The Christian Science Monitor*. Retrieved October 3, 2010 (http://www.csmonitor.com/2006/1019/p15s01-legn.html).

Thurau, Lisa H., and Johanna Wald. 2010. Controlling Partners: When Law Enforcement Meets Discipline in Public Schools. *New York Law School Law Review* 54: 977–1020.

Times Wire Reports. February 1, 2001. "Child Suspended for Brandishing Chicken." Retrieved September 20, 2010 (http://articles.latimes.com/2001/feb/01/news/mn-19819).

Trembley, Richard E. and Wendy M. Craig. 1995. "Developmental Crime Prevention." *Crime and Justice* 19: 151–236.

Trump, Kenneth S. (No Date). National School Safety and Security Services. "School Associated Violent Deaths and School Shootings." Retrieved July 15, 2010 (http://www.schoolsecurity.org/trends/school_violence.html).

Turvey, Brent E. 2008. *Criminal Profiling: An Introduction to Behavioral Evidence Analysis, 3rd Edition*. Burlington, MA: Academic Press.

Twemlow, Stuart W., Peter Fonagy, Frank C. Sacco, Mary Ellen O'Toole, and Eric Vernberg. 2002. "Premeditated Mass Shootings in Schools: Threat Assessment." *Journal of the American Academy of Child and Adolescent Psychiatry* 41(4): 475–477.

Twemlow, Stuart W., Peter Fonagy, and Frank C. Sacco. 2004. "The Role of the Bystander in the Social Architecture of Bullying and Violence in Schools and Communities." *Annals of the New York Academy of Sciences* 1036: 215–232.

Urbina, Ian. October 11, 2009. "It's a Fork, It's a Spoon, It's a... Weapon." *New York Times*. Retrieved October 3, 2010 (http://www.nytimes.com/2009/10/12/education/12discipline.html?_r=2).

Van Ness, Daniel W., and Karen Heetderks Strong. 2010. *Restoring Justice: An Introduction to Restorative Justice*. New Providence, NJ: Anderson.

Verhovek, Sam Howe. November 11, 1999. "Teenager to Spend Life in Prison For Shootings." Retrieved April 13, 2012 (http://www.nytimes.com/1999/11/11/us/teenager-to-spend-life-in-prison-for-shootings.html?ref=kiplandfkinkel).

Verlinden, Stephanie, Michel Hersen, and Jay Thomas. 2000. "Risk Factors in School Shootings." *Clinical Psychology Review* 20(1): 3–56.

Vincent, Gina M., Anna M. Terry, and Shannon M. Maney. 2009. "Risk/Needs Tools for Antisocial Behavior and Violence Among Youthful Populations." Pp. 377–424 in *Handbook of Violence Risk Assessment and Treatment: New Approaches for Mental Health Professionals*, edited by Joel T. Andrade. New York, NY: Springer.

138 References

Virginia Tech Review Panel. 2007. "Mass Shootings at Virginia Tech April 16, 2007: Report of the Virginia Tech Review Panel presented to Timothy M. Kaine, Governor, Commonwealth of Virginia." Retrieved April 10, 2012 (http://www.vtreviewpanel.org/report/index.html).

Volokh, Alexander. 2000. "A Brief Guide to School-Violence Prevention." *Journal of Law and Family Studies* 2(2): 99–152.

Vossekuil, Bryan, Robert Fein, Marissa Reddy, Randy Borum, and William Modzeleski. 2002. "The Final Report and Findings of the Safe School Initiative: Implications for the Prevention of School Attacks in the United States." Washington, DC: U.S. Secret Service and U.S. Department of Education.

Wacquant, Loïc. 2009. *Punishing the Poor: The Neoliberal Government of Social Insecurity*. Durham, NC: Duke University Press.

Wald, Johanna, and Daniel J. Losen. 2003. "Editors' Notes." Pp. 1–2 in *New Directions for Youth Development: Deconstructing the School-to-Prison Pipeline*, edited by Johanna Wald and Daniel J. Losen. San Francisco, CA: Jossey-Bass.

Watkins, Adam M. 2005. "Examining the Disparity between Juvenile and Adult Victims in Notifying the Police: A Study of Mediating Variables." *Journal of Research in Crime and Delinquency* 42(3): 333–353.

Watts, Ivan E., and Nirmala Erevelles. 2004. "These Deadly Times: Reconceptualizing School Violence by Using Critical Race Theory and Disability Studies." *American Educational Research Journal* 41(2): 271–299.

Webber, Julie A. 2003. *Failure to Hold: The Politics of School Violence*. New York: Rowman & Littlefield Publishers.

Western, Bruce. 2007. *Punishment and Inequality in America*. New York: Russell Sage.

White-Hamon, Laura Suzanne. 2000. "Mass Murder and Attempted Mass Murder: An Examination of the Perpetrator with an Empirical Analysis of Typologies." Unpublished Doctoral Dissertation. California School of Professional Psychology, Fresno, CA.

Whitehead, John W. January 23, 2001. "Zero Common Sense School Discipline Rules Cheapen Students' Humanity." *The Rutherford Institute*. Retrieved September 20, 2010 (http://www.rutherford.org/articles_db/commentary.asp?record_id=99).

Wilson-Simmons, Renee, Kimberly Dash, Parisa Tehranifar, Lydia O'Donnell, and Ann Stueve. 2006. "What Can Student Bystanders

Do to Prevent School Violence? Perceptions of Students and Staff." *Journal of School Violence* 5(1): 43–62.
Wise, Tim. 2001. "School Shootings and White Denial." *Multicultural Perspectives* 3(4): 3–4.
Wylie, Lindsey E., Chris L. Gibson, Eve M. Brank, Mark R. Fondacaro, Stephen W. Smith, Veda E. Brown, and Scott A. Miller. 2010. "Assessing School and Student Predictors of Weapons Reporting." *Youth Violence and Juvenile Justice October* 8(4): 351–372.
Yaffe, Gideon. 2010. *Attempts: In the Philosophy of Action and the Criminal Law*. New York: Oxford University Press.
Young, Jock. 1994. "Incessant Chatter: Recent Paradigms in Criminology." Pp. 69–124 in *The Oxford Handbook of Criminology*, edited by Mike Maguire, Rod Morgan, and Robert Reiner. Oxford: Oxford University Press.
Youth Justice Board. 2004. "National Evaluation of the Restorative Justice in Schools Programme." Retrieved February 24, 2014 (http://www.restorativejustice.org.uk/resource/national_evaluation_of_the_restorative_justice_in_schools_programme/).

Index

actuarial justice, 18–22, 66–68, 100
American Bar Association, 12, 24
American Psychological Association, 12, 15, 24
April 20th, 28–29, 37
arming faculty members, 101–102
attempted crime, 102–103
automated decision making, 15–16
averted school rampage, 8–11, 31, 108

breaking the code of silence, 78–84, 88–89
bombs, 4, 9, 28, 33, 35–36, 38–39, 41–42, 52, 54, 84, 107, 113
bullying, 7, 10, 22, 51, 93
bystander intervention, 70, 72–73, 78–84, 88–94, 97
bystander inaction, 84–86

Chardon High School massacre, 99
Columbine High School massacre, 4, 7, 29, 32–33, 37, 41–42, 51–54, 63, 70–75, 84–85, 102, 107
Columbine Report, 53
copycat effect, 53–54

crime prevention through environmental design, 13
criminal attempts, 102–103

depression/suicidal thinking, 7, 34, 36, 47–49, 59, 81
deterrence, 21–22, 71, 87, 92, 94, 97, 101, 103
deviant group/subcultural affiliation, 51–53
directly informed confidants, 79–80

false accusations, 99–100
fascination with rampage violence, 53–54
Friday the 13th, 52
Foucault, Michel, 21, 99

gender, 8, 44–46, 54, 60
generalizability, 58, 100, 114–116
Giffords, Gabrielle, 102
Goth subculture, 34, 51–53
grounded theory, 115
group characteristics, 32, 43, 49–53, 66, 96–97
guided professional judgment, *See* warning signs
gun availability, 8, 32, 38–40, 102
gun control, 101–102

Harcourt, Bernard, 19
Harris, Eric, 32, 53–54

Index 141

hit list, 5, 28–30, 33, 35–36, 59–61, 78–79, 114
homogeneous communities, 8
Hymowitz, Kay, 24

indirectly informed bystanders, 78–79
individual characteristics, *See* personal characteristics
international comparative research, 101–102
involved co-conspirators, 80–83, 94

killer duos, 102
Klebold, Dylan, 32, 53–54

Lanza, Adam, 71
leakage, 71, 78–94
lockdown drills, 2, 75
Louisiana Technical College massacre, 44

marginalization, 49–51
masculinity, 8, 44–46
mass murder, 6, 10, 32, 43, 102–103, 106–107
mental illness/mental health issues, 7, 47–49, 51, 60
metal detectors, 13, 22, 71, 76, 87, 97, 100

Nazi skinhead subculture, 51–53
Natural Born Killers, 54
neoliberal penality, 19–21

personal characteristics, 43–49, 53–54, 66, 96–97
planning a rampage attack, 31–43
positive school climate, 75–78, 82–83, 87, 90–94, 97, 100
previous history of misbehavior, 46–47
profiling, 14–15, 62–63

qualitative methodology, 57–58, 101, 109, 114–116

race/ethnicity, 43–44, 54, 113
Red Lake Senior High School massacre, 43, 71
restorative justice, 22, 92–94, 97, 100
restorative classroom discipline, 22, 93–94, 97, 100
risk
  levels of, 16–17, 29–30
risk society, 20–21

Sandy Hook Elementary School massacre, 71
school criminalization
  causes of, 18–22
  definition of, 2, 91
school rampage
  causes of, 7–8
  definition of, 6, 105–108
school resource officers (SROs), 2, 12, 35–37, 71, 77, 82–83, 87
school-to-prison pipeline, 99
social status at school, 49–53
sociology of risk, 99
student code of silence, 70–94, 97–100, 103
student/faculty rapport, 74, 77–78
substantive threats, 16–17, 30, 58, 62, 64, 105
surveillance cameras, 2, 11–13, 18, 22, 71, 76, 87, 97, 100
suspicious clothing, 51–53

Tasso de Silveira Municipal School massacre, 43
threat
  forms of (verbal, written, and electronic), 28–29
threat assessment approach, 16–18
threatened targets, 80
transferability, 116
transient threats, 17, 30, 38, 105
trench coats, 9, 51–52

victims, targeted vs. random, 33–36
violence risk assessment, 13–18

DOI: 10.1057/9781137399281.0010

violent media/music, 51
Virginia Tech massacre, 29, 43

warning signs, 15, 42–54, 66
weapons
   acquisition, possession, and/or manufacture of, 32, 39–40, 43
   fascination with, 42–43
   training with, 32, 40–43
Weise, Jeffrey, 71
Westside Middle School massacre, 102
Williams, Latina, 44

zero tolerance policies, 11–12, 24–25, 57, 61, 68, 71, 87, 91–94, 98

CPSIA information can be obtained
at www.ICGtesting.com
Printed in the USA
LVHW052049231119
638281LV00022B/1264/P

9 781349 486465